1-14-60

SECRETS OF ANSWERED PRAYER

SECRETS OF
ANSWERED PRAYER

Cyril H. Powell

THOMAS Y. CROWELL COMPANY

New York • Established 1834

DEDICATED TO

The Southfields Wednesday Night Fellowship

"No one believes in answered prayer more than I do, yet I stand here to announce a seeming paradox, and that is that none of *my* prayers has ever been answered. None of your prayers is ever answered. *Only God's prayers are answered.* Only as you and I succeed in making our prayers God's prayers are they ever answered. Once succeed in doing that and they are *always* answered."

GLENN CLARK

INTRODUCTION

Ask, and it shall be given you; seek, and ye shall find; knock, and it shall be opened unto you.

MATTHEW 7: 7

TOWARDS the end of his life, Steinmetz, the great electrical engineer, made a surprising statement—that is, a surprising statement coming from a man with his background. He was asked from what direction he expected the greatest discoveries of the future would be made. When he spoke, atomic fission was still a dream. Man had not yet launched artificial satellites into outer space. All manner of scientific discoveries were at hand. Instead, however, of venturing into prophecies concerning matters of that kind he spoke, very deliberately, of something quite different.

"I think," he said, "that the greatest discoveries will be made along spiritual lines. Here is a force which history clearly teaches has been the greatest power in the development of men and history. Yet we have been merely playing with it and have never seriously studied it as we have the physical forces. . . ." And then, beginning to speak of what he thought might happen when this "serious study" should start, he went on, "Then the scientists of the world will turn their laboratories over to the study of God and prayer and the spiritual forces which as yet have hardly been scratched. When this day comes," he prophesied, "the world will see more advancement in one generation than it has seen in the last four."

Now this is a scientist talking, and his language is not, perhaps, the language that you or I would use. But what a

7

fascinating picture his words bring to mind! A picture of scientists proceeding on a systematic study of prayer and the forces which govern it. It is a somewhat fantastic picture, however, for prayer is hardly a force capable of being exercised in the dispassionate way of the scientist, and instruments for measuring it would need to be most unusually contrived! So much with which it has to do would be totally out of place in a scientist's laboratory. At the same time, Steinmetz was right in thinking that it is something with which to make experiments, and right, too, in thinking that some of its results can be verified. It is also true that it acts according to what might be called "laws". There are consistencies in its operation.

But what this scientist seemed to ignore is that across the centuries men *have* been using it, and experimenting with it in many ways. We have had—and still have—our spiritual explorers. This has been true from the time of Abraham, the "friend of God", to Elijah who, as St. James expressed it, "prayed in his prayer", on to our Lord Himself, and to countless disciples who have followed Him in this path. Their "laboratory" has been the life of the world, and the results of their praying have indeed affected its history. Perhaps we have not been systematic enough in learning from them; and most certainly we have been giving the impression, so far as spiritual power is concerned, that we have not "seriously studied it" as men have "the physical forces": many of us, in Steinmetz's words, have "merely been playing with it".

In this book we set out to do two things. One is to attempt to discover some of the underlying "laws" of prayer, and to do this by investigating the lives and experiences of some of its great exponents. We shall not, in this study, be examining Bible characters. That has been done quite recently by R. E. O. White in his book, *They Teach Us to Pray*[1] (it was, actually, the perusal of this book that acted as the trigger to start the

[1] Published by Arthur James (Evesham).

present author on this one!). We shall discover that some of these people, from the very earliest days, were amazingly "scientific" in their attitude towards these matters. Some, indeed, have actually conducted what could be called "experiments" in connection with it. That strange—and to some of us rather unlovely—character, George Müller, is a case in point. I wonder how many know that he started out on the development and maintenance of his orphanages not so much out of concern for the orphans as in order to demonstrate that *without visible resources so vast an undertaking could be supported by faith and prayer alone*? The experiment so succeeded that nearly two million pounds were drawn from the public to support a work run in England by a Prussian, whose method was not to issue financial appeals, but to pray believingly to God. Müller's work is so often referred to that we shall not examine it here: but we shall look for evidence as authentic and experimental.

The second thing is that we shall stimulate one another to venture in these realms. Our examination will be conducted in that spirit. We hope that many people whose prayers have lacked vitality, and many who have been puzzled by what they consider to be lack of "answers" to their own prayers, may find light and encouragement as we proceed. Not every chapter will mean as much to every one as some other will do. In these realms what is the way for one is not necessarily the way for another.

We shall gather our materials chiefly from biographical and autobiographical sources, spending most of our time in our own century, listening to some of our contemporaries who at this moment are busy in the great laboratory of the world, endeavouring to serve God and their fellows, and who thus are working at this subject of prayer in a live and practical fashion. Our one rule, as we set out, is that we shall follow the line of the "discoverers" and "explorers" in these matters.

It is possible to translate the well-known sentence in James

5 in this way, "The supplication of a man who is right with God is very powerful because it is divinely energised." When we think of our Lord Himself, it is quite clear that for Him prayer was the gateway to spiritual power. He, indeed, is its supreme exponent, and no one has said more daring things about it than He. "Ask," He says, "and it shall be given you; seek, and ye shall find; knock, and it shall be opened unto you." Evidently, He found that things worked that way.

These men and women whom we shall consider never went beyond their Lord in any of their discoveries. What they do is to help to draw out some of the things embedded in His teaching and experience. They are men and women who learned to pray by praying. They can help us to start where we are, and how we are, or, if we have already gone some distance ourselves on this path, to venture further.

Among all these masters, I would like to know how authentic "Billy Hicks" happens to be. For me, he stands for the beginner in prayer who, because of his very simplicity, and because of his need, at one bound takes a long stride into the territory of prayer. I have known one or two like him. You remember his story?

In the old sailing ship days, an officer from a sister ship coming aboard a man-o'-war asked the captain, "Have you a man called Hicks? I'd like to see him." When Hicks arrived, the officer began to read from a little notebook he carried. Hicks went red in the face. On a dark night, the officer had seen lights flashing. He had read them, and it was these signals that he was reading from his book.

"You're making fun of me, sir," said Billy Hicks.

"No, I'm not," replied the officer, "but tell me about it."

"It was like this, sir. I was made captain of the foretop, after two of my mates had missed their footing up there, and been killed. I was in a funk. I asked the officer if I might go to the tops and practise some signalling. He let me go.

When I got my light going, I just said my prayers with it. That's all, sir."

"Good man!" commented the officer. This is what he had "overheard", as he read the lights on that dark night, "God this is Billy Hicks signalling. I've bin promoted Cap of the Foretop. God, I'm frightened. God, I ain't much feared of death, but, Your Holiness, when I go up tomorrow give me nerve to play the man. And, God, give me what I used to feel when I knelt at my mother's knee and said, 'Our Father'. Good night, God. Yours truly Billy Hicks."

Maybe the story of how the captain of the foretop got his nerve deserves to be recorded in the lists of the experiments in prayer already conducted in the laboratory of the world. It was a prayer made in a way, and in a language, real to the man who prayed it, and it was answered.

In the nature of the case, so much of one's praying is impossible to follow up so that one can say, "this was the prayer" and "this was the answer". But there are times when the praying has been of an intimate, specific kind—for this person, or that thing, *now*. And one has voiced the prayer at a time when adventitious circumstances could not enter. Then one *knew* the fact of the answer when it came.

All of us who over the years have prayed have our assurances concerning answered prayer. Sometimes we have asked amiss. Sometimes our heart has not been in the prayer we have prayed with our lips. Sometimes we have asked in unbelief, doubting. Sometimes we have sought our own will, and not the will of God. Yet an answer has come. Sometimes it has been a plain "No", and after a while we have come to recognize that as as definite an answer as any other. If our struggling and trying, in the meanwhile, has brought us to a closer knowledge of God, and of ourselves, then our prayer has been answered in another way, too. Sometimes the answer has been "Wait", and waiting patiently for God and in God, we have seen Him accomplish His purposes in ways that, possibly, were quite different from the ways we expected when we first prayed our prayer.

Together we are setting out to discover some of the secrets of answered prayer. It is a fair question, since we shall be looking so much at other people's lives and experiences, to ask if the author himself knows anything of answers. The reply would be, "Thanks be to God, yes, again and again. Not as much, and not as often, as might be, because some of the lessons at which we shall be looking have not been fully learned. But often enough—in a positive way—for him to know that, when one masters the secret, or rather is mastered by the Master, prayer is always answered."

It is difficult to give some of the instances which have made the deepest impression because they involve other people and circumstances which, because of their nature, should be kept private.

Here are just two instances that will guide us as we proceed. When I was a young Christian, full of faith and enthusiasm, my mother fell seriously ill. I prayed earnestly, and my prayer was one prayer—that she should recover. As she continued in hospital, there came a time when the specialist had to say to us, "There is no hope". But this was not accepted by the young Christian. Hadn't Jesus said to Jairus, "Be not afraid. Only believe"? Hadn't He said that whatsoever we ask in faith, believing, would be granted? Wasn't this report of the physicians but one more test of faith? So I continued, more fervently than ever, to pray. My mind, I am sure, looking back, was not divided in this. I really did believe that the miracle of which the specialist spoke ("only a miracle can save her") would happen. Over a period of about a fortnight, I prayed like this, and every night during that time I saw my mother for a minute or two, for we were allowed to visit her at any time. There came an evening when my brother and I went to see her. I cannot tell you exactly how it happened, but that night I *knew*—I knew that my mother was not to get better, and that this was all in the providence of God. When I got outside I did what I hadn't done until then, I broke down. And when I got home, with my fit of crying over, I prayed in an altogether new way. My prayer now was that God would make her passing easy, and that He would receive her unto Himself. The prayer, in other words, was changed, and that not by me. I *knew* that this was the right prayer to pray now.

For an hour or so, I went for a walk with a friend. When we returned, my brother's car was ready at the door. . . . It all happened as I had prayed. Her passing, after the stiff fight of the last weeks and months, was full of peace. Our beloved minister was with her when it happened, and he was there because messengers had gone with the news of her relapse to the church where we would normally have been for a meeting. The last words she heard were these: "Yea, though I walk through the valley of the shadow of death, I will fear no evil, for thou art with me." I am sure that it was like that for her.

Later, much later, this son of hers was a Methodist minister, living at Gateshead-on-Tyne. For a special occasion or two he had gone across the river to a church in Newcastle. "You know," he said to his wife on his return from these visits, "that's just the sort of church I'd like to go to." Nothing more was said to her or anybody else. One day, like a bolt out of the blue, came the information that the present minister of that church was leaving: "Would you like to come?" It seemed the answer to my deepest desiring, which as H. E. Fosdick used to say, is our real prayer. At that stage nothing was put into writing. It was assumed that I would go, and that when the time came the formalities would be gone through without any trouble. I thought so, too. Then, when that time approached things began to happen. On every occasion when I was about to say "Yes", a stop came in the way. First, a

Congregational minister, whose opinion I much respected, volunteered to advise me not to go. His reasons seemed slender, but his advice was given most strongly. On another occasion, when I was on the point of writing a letter of acceptance, the telephone bell rang and the stewards of the church to which I finally went wanted to know if I would consider an invitation to go there. As my wife and I said to one another after the third or fourth stop of this kind, "It's uncanny". I felt I understood for myself the kind of thing that St. Luke portrays in Acts 16, where he tells of Paul's coming to Troas and the crossing of the gospel to Europe: "Forbidden of the Holy Spirit to preach the word in Asia, after that they were come to Mysia, they assayed to go into Bithynia: but the Spirit suffered them not." Though my exploits weren't in the least comparable, the negative guidance that we received was. It was an answer to the prayer we were praying: "Lord, we want to take the next step that you want", and the plain fact was that it wasn't the step we had first thought of, nor the way that had first opened.

Answers come: help, blessing, guidance, understanding, influence upon the lives of others. What we want to discover are more of the secrets that lie behind this.

One further thing needs to be said, by way of introduction. It will only be possible, in what follows, to indicate certain broad main lines of investigation. We shall attempt to single out, in each chapter, some particular contribution made by the person in question. No one must imagine that this, or indeed the rest of what we shall be able to say about them in the compass of one short chapter, is the limit of what these "masters" in the realm of prayer have to say to us. Many will want to learn more concerning them, and to discover more of their teaching. One of our hopes is that this book will serve, in many instances, as an introduction to the books from which we shall be quoting.

1958.   CYRIL H. POWELL.

CONTENTS

HORIZONS BEFORE US

THE FINAL SECRET

1. HUGH REDWOOD

Exploring the Power of Prayer

With God all things are possible.

MARK 10: 27

"WOULDN'T YOU like to do some exploring?" It was just before eight on a Wednesday morning in August 1950, and the radio set was switched on in the other room. The strong Bristolian voice continued, "Wouldn't you like to collect the evidence for the Kingdom? Wouldn't it make your everyday life a different thing altogether if you began to assemble proofs of a power able, *in* you and *with* you and *through* you, to bring things to pass which you once would have called miracles? I'm talking of things like providence, guidance, healing; the meeting of all manner of needs. I have seen these things for myself . . . I believe God wants us to undertake this exploration."

As I listened I knew that my answer to these questions was, "Yes", and I could not have agreed more with the speaker that our Lord invites us to embark with Him on a lifetime adventure of spiritual exploration.

It is remarkable how certain radio speakers immediately seem to establish an intimacy. It was so with this speaker. I felt I knew him. Actually, I did in a second-hand sort of manner. I had once written to him, asking of him a service, and I had had a gracious letter in reply. I had read all his books, beginning with that most stimulating first book, *God*

17

in the Slums. Each of these books, down to the latest, written in 1957, echoes this invitation to adventure in prayer, and to discover spiritual law for oneself.

Hugh Redwood, for it was his voice that I had been listening to on that August morning, has told us how his Christian life really began when, in 1927, he switched on a radio set which he had just constructed, and heard a voice, rich and deep, that seemed to be sounding in the same room with him. This voice, oddly enough, was also speaking about prayer. The Fleet Street night editor of the *Daily News* was gripped by what he heard.

It is the fact of prayer, and the thought of prayer that spans the years. The fact that H.R. is still with us is not unconnected with it. His latest book, which, not inaptly, he entitles *Residue of Days*, tells how, in August 1956, at the age of seventy-three, he was taken into hospital for an intestinal operation. The first operation was "exploratory", revealing the need for a further drastic operation involving a colostomy. Given no more than two days to make up his mind—for the matter was urgent— Hugh Redwood faced the matter quietly with God. The operation would have been of such a nature, he says, that if it did not kill him outright, it would have been impossible for him to resume the kind of work to which he felt called.

His own doctor—who, by the way, had come to see him at the outset of this trouble without being sent for—at his request joined in the consultation with the surgeon. The X-ray films were produced and interpreted. The obstructing cancer was now the size of an orange. When the surgeon knew of Redwood's decision not to have the operation he said, "In my opinion, you are making a very grave mistake". "As your doctor," said the other, "it is my duty to tell you that, if you do not have the operation, I shall not expect to find you alive at Christmas."

Then the latter, having said this on the purely medical level, added, as he explained the position to the surgeon, "You must try to understand this man as I do. He lives in two worlds at once, and I think he feels at home in both, so that the question of life or death doesn't weigh with him overmuch as a personal matter. It's a case for his conscience, and, knowing the facts, I don't see how he could reach any other decision."

That was on August 21st, with Christmas only a few months away. But, says Redwood, from that time "life steadily returned to normal. In a week I was back on a healthy man's diet: in a month I was speaking in public again. And there is a note in my diary to remind me that on Sept. 18 I ordered my Christmas cards and bought my new year's engagement-book".

The doctor's report of what happened is a remarkable document. It reveals that the surgeon stressed that, if the operation were not performed, H.R. would have to return within a few days for an emergency one. "For the first time in my life," writes the doctor, "I have witnessed, in this healing, a Divine miracle. In fact, I feel almost as if I had been face-to-face with the Creator himself."

Between those two events—the sermon on Prayer in 1927, and the healing in 1956—Hugh Redwood has been able, in his own words, to assemble any number of "proofs of a power able, *in* you and *with* you and *through* you, to bring things to pass which you once would have called miracles".

For example, in his book, *Practical Prayer*, he tells of an occasion in the 1930's, when travelling on the Lord's business, he and his friends were marvellously set on their way. Details are there, too, of remarkable conjunctions and "coincidences" by which the needs of one person, and the generosity of a quite-unknown third-party, have answered one another, H.R. acting as the "clearing-house" between them. The whole transaction took place in the atmosphere of prayer.

His latest book records the story of a car journey back from Bath to London. Fog came down, and continuation of the journey seemed virtually impossible. A lorry overtook the car, announcing the fact by putting on its lights. Once in front, it slowed down, as if giving an invitation to follow. The un-known, but most skilful lorry driver piloted them through the fog right from Newbury to London, until the very moment when, in Knightsbridge, it lifted. H.R. wrote to the "District Nurse" (as she is known, through her radio programmes), who had organised the meeting which they had attended at the far end. Their letters crossed. These were the opening words of hers: "Some of us, at this end, had little sleep last night. We were awake, praying you safely home through the fog. I do trust that all was well, and you landed in safely, blessing the Hand that guided."

As illustrating the continuance of the "clearing-house" pattern, he tells how, in the summer of 1957 he felt it right to do something for friends feeling the pinch of present difficulties. Some few years ago, at Christmas, he had felt similarly led to send a gift from the "clearing-house" to a friend in the West Country (the gifts come from people content that they should be used at his discretion), who was asked, by means of it, to give gifts of coal to needy people at Christmastime. It was most appreciated. This time, in early summer 1957, with coal prices about to rise, Hugh Redwood felt that friends nearer home needed the same kind of help. There were not ample funds in the clearing-house, but friendly coal-merchants co-operated in the scheme, and on July 16th, H.R. sent them his cheque. *On the same day*, July 16th, this time it was the West Country friend who sent him a letter, beginning: "Now it is my turn to send *you* something. . . ."

Hugh Redwood's story, set out in his full-scale book, *Bristol Fashion*, is the story of a Bristol boy who became a reporter, first on a local paper, and then in London. In 1901, while in Bristol, he passed through a conversion experience. Its influence did not last and, looking back, he lists three reasons for this: (1) too much publicity; (2) absence of teaching in prayer; (3) and the failure to relate "holiness"—he was converted in the Salvation Army—to daily work.

Truly, says the author, it is astonishing that a young convert should fail, in an organisation like the Salvation Army, to receive help and instruction in how to pray. "But in how many churches or chapels," he pertinently asks, "is any prayer teaching given?" What he now knows he needed, and what he says would also have given him the key to "holiness", was instruction in communion with God.

The intervening twenty-six years, though full of event and interest were empty of religion, until that fateful day when the dial of the new radio set was turned, and the voice of W. H. Elliott came from the instrument, speaking about prayer. This time what happened really was a new beginning. And something had occurred which was only just in time.

Within a few days, Hugh's daughter, Gwen, nearing seventeen, and about to leave her City of London School, was stricken by infantile paralysis. There was a power now to quiet the panic that H.R. felt rising in his soul. He tells us that when he heard the doctor's voice telling him that it was polio, and that the girl's life was in danger, it seemed as if, corresponding to the wildness of the night outside, evil powers were unleashed within him. It was the fact of another Presence that stilled that storm, he tells us; and in that same hour he knew that his daughter would not die. It was actually at that very time that, in the hospital, her temperature dropped from 104.6 to 99, and her fever abated.

The next year was the year of the Thameside floods, and H.R., now night editor of the *Daily News*, went down to see what was happening. There, once again, he came into contact with the Salvation Army, and what he saw, and the way that it stirred him, formed the basis of his first book, *God in the Slums*. The book led to all manner of things—invitations to preach, appeals for help, and finally to H.R.'s appointment as Religious Editor of the *News Chronicle* (the successor to the *Daily News*). This was a new type of appointment in Fleet Street, and well and worthily did H.R. discharge it. Thus did this Anglican layman become the friend of all the churches.

Meanwhile, Edith, Hugh Redwood's wife, passed through one period of ill-health after another, until finally on January 1st, 1939, she died of cancer. Now one can see how providential it was that Canon Elliott's sermon in 1927, which had awakened Hugh Redwood, had been about prayer. This second conversion, unlike the first, was lasting because prayer had been built into it.

"But for the sermon on prayer through which my life was changed," he says himself, "I should have entered upon this dark period with no experience whatever of prayer as I now understand it. As it was, prayer gave us our only hope, slender indeed at the start, when I could do little more than cry, 'Lord, I believe, help Thou my unbelief', but increasingly firm as that cry was heard and answered. Help came through all manner of channels, and more and more through the ever widening fellowship of believers to which *God in the Slums* admitted me." H.R. has been fortunate, not only in his own discoveries and adventures in prayer, but in the gathering round him of faithful, praying people—this through his newspaper work, his books, his preaching, his radio messages and his personal contacts.

What then has this man specially to say to us about the secrets of answered prayer? He has, indeed, so much to say that one must recommend all interested to read his own books, and especially *Practical Prayer* and *Residue of Days*. Among the many things that Canon Elliott said in that broadcast sermon which caught the listening ear of the man from Fleet Street was that prayer ought to be systematic and practical. Why not, for instance, use a card-index as a help to the memory, and to introduce business-like methods into prayer? In H.R.'s study, the card-index used in his morning praying over the years has a place of honour. Equally insistent with this idea of making prayer a business-like transaction is Hugh Redwood's concern to encourage spiritual adventurers and explorers. Christians, he says, know all-too-little about the outworking of spiritual laws.

What he covets for the churches is the rediscovery of the power of prayer, and the desire to experiment with it. Scientifically, and systematically, praying groups should adventure into its uses. "Were I appointed minister of a church," he writes, "I should want to know first of all if regular meetings were held for prayer. If so, I should want to make certain that they were run upon business-like lines: if not, and indeed, in any case, I should open a school of prayer in a spirit of high adventure." The surest way to revival, he considers, lies in this direction.

Regarding prayer and its answering, these are what he summarises as bed-rock truths:

(1) No honest prayer offered to God can ever be without result.

(2) The measure in which its specific requests are fulfilled depends upon the extent to which those desires are consonant with the purposes of God.

(3) "Subject to this reservation there is nothing which prayer cannot accomplish, when it is rightly understood and practised."

Here is a man who has proved these truths in his own experience over a long period of years. Shall we learn from him to make our prayers real, experimental—more business-like and practical, knowing that God wishes us to engage upon this adventure of prayer? We shall learn in Christ's school as we go forward. "Jesus bids us seek," says H.R., "and seeking implies research, and research experiment and test." Here, in terms of this man's life, as well as his teaching, we are invited to go forward.

2. EDWIN ORR

ADVENTURING IN FAITH

*Commit thy way unto the Lord; trust also in him, and he shall
bring it to pass.*

PSALM 37: 5

FOR A SHORT, but most interesting, period of years I was
on the teaching staff of a College in Derbyshire to which
men came for a year's training in Bible Study and Evangelism.

One evening, I remember one of these young men, an
engaging son of Northern Ireland, telling us how he came to
the College. First, he felt it was in the Lord's will. But how
could he come without resources? In his breezy style and Irish
brogue, he told us how he prayed about it. One of the things
he needed was a portmanteau. So he "pra-ayed" about it.
Sure enough, a woman offered him a brand-new one within
a day or two. There was something else he needed. Sure
enough, it came too. As I listened, I felt nauseated. The Lord
seemed to have been reduced, in this young man's eyes, to a
sort of telephone clearing agency for his particular wants! It
seemed to me—perhaps a little cynically—as if on his part he
had perfected a method of "sponging" on people. I hasten
to add that the man of whom I tell this recounted these things,
as I believe, in a sincere spirit, but he was very immature then,
and his way of reporting what had happened, punctuated as
it was with bursts of laughter from many of his hearers,
affected a number of others of them in the way I have indicated.

24

With every year since he has matured, and he is a splendid evangelist now.

I wondered, however, what was the origin of this particular method and this particular style. A little later I was to discover.

It was at about the same time that my little second-hand car finally announced its intention to serve me no more. Situated as we were in the heart of Derbyshire, and having to journey often on preaching engagements, I really did need a car. "Why don't you pray about it?" said one of the students, and then added with a grin, "But be sure you pray in the right place, and with the right kind of people to hear you." Again, a particular method of going about things was being "guyed". No wonder people became cynical about the cadging-by-prayer method that some folk have employed.

All this is by way of preamble to what is to follow. I am anxious not to encourage anybody in a career of praying for cars, or for portmanteaus, or for anything else that had far better come to them through normal channels. You will see that I have a natural abhorrence of anything that savours of treating God as a sort of butler who opens the heavenly larder whenever we call, or as a super-telephone operator who connects our appeal with a suitable donor. Yet, having said that, I do believe that Paul was right when he wrote to the Philippians, "My God shall supply all your need according to his riches in glory by Christ Jesus." I *know* that God supports His own when they are sent out on *His* missions. I know the story of George Müller, and now I know the story of Edwin Orr. It was when I read this latter story that I knew I was at the fountain source of many imitations—especially from Northern Ireland!

I think a George Müller and an Edwin Orr every so often help us to see, on a large and very obvious scale, that God means what He says in His promises. These people try them out in a thoroughgoing and dramatic fashion that is not necessarily meant to provide a pattern for anybody else. They themselves are careful to point out that they were led to this by God. You, if you try anything remotely similar, will need to be as sure that you are!

It was in August 1933, when about twenty, that our young Irishman, Edwin Orr, was invited to go to London to join "a Christian organisation". It meant leaving his secular employment. The salary that was offered would, however, enable him to continue the support he was giving to his widowed mother. By that time, Edwin was the leader of an enthusiastic group of Belfast street preachers and youth group evangelists who had come into being through prayer, and who were, at that very period, praying that Edwin should be released from home duties for just some such work as this.

Unfortunately the man responsible for giving him the invitation to full-time service left the country, and the committee of the organisation in question did not uphold it. Impulsive young Edwin, in the meanwhile, had left his job. The effect of the disappointment at first, as he tells us, was shattering. It was then that he made his decision to venture out without the financial backing of any organisation. He was to risk himself and his future in simple dependence upon God.

"But what will become of us?" his mother asked, not unnaturally.

"I don't know, Mother. But I promise to send you the usual contribution I give you every week, less ten shillings for my own food."

"I know you'll try. But where will it come from?"

"I don't know. But it says in the Bible, 'My God shall supply all your need' and either that's true or else it's not. If it's true, we'll be all right; if it's not true, the sooner we find out the better. But of course it's true."

And with no more than that spirit of faith and adventure, and the haziest of ideas of what he was going to do and where he was going—except that he felt called to "stir up interest in a spiritual awakening all over the world"—he left home, equipped with a ticket to Liverpool, which had been supplied by "a gentleman in Belfast", an old bicycle and the sum of two shillings and eightpence farthing in his pocket. All his friends, as he says, thought him crazy.

Thus began a journey which took him the length and breadth of Britain. It was, mainly, undertaken on the old bicycle, until this was replaced by the gift of a new one which—like everything else about this trip—was offered just at the time of need!

As the intrepid Irishman pedalled first to Chester, then on to Shrewsbury, and so on in this remarkable itinerary, friends were found and friends were made. Let Edwin tell, for example, of what happened when he reached Shrewsbury at eleven p.m. on the second night of the journey, with nowhere to go. A policeman who happened to be about was asked where cheap lodgings could be found.

"What do you do for a living?" the constable asked.

On being told that the stranger was "an evangelist", he smiled. "Can you prove that?" In his pocket, Edwin had letters of introduction and from them he chose one. It was from the least-well-known sponsor among them. The policeman looked at the signature, and smiled more broadly than ever. "This William Phillips who's written this glowing letter about you is a friend of mine," he explained. And lodgings for the night were secure!

It so happened, by the way, that this story was later checked by A. J. Russell. It was then that Constable Maule disclosed the fact that that night, because of a mistake he had made on his beat, he had retraced his steps. His meeting with Edwin Orr at that spot would never have occurred in the ordinary way!

On his journeying, Edwin met with Christian pastors and evangelists who invited him to join their work and campaigning, or to talk to their young people's meetings. All the time he managed to send the promised money to his mother, as well as to find his own needs met. He had by now a little room which had been placed at his disposal in Fleet Street. One day, when he returned to his pied-à-terre, he had no money to send to her, nor for several days thereafter. Then, he tells us, there "came a letter written by a comparative stranger, saying that he had wanted to write to me, but, being unable to reach me, he sent the amount as a gift to my mother instead, using the address in Belfast that certain friends of mine had used before I had started out. Imagine my surprise when I discovered that he had sent exactly the amount needed for two weeks' support of the home".

In all this, the young evangelist was proving that God was fulfilling His promise, and providing for his needs. Concerning the first three months of this kind of adventuring, Edwin writes: "I had avoided letting anyone know of any specific need, and yet when the answer to prayer had come, it was so specific that one could not doubt that it came from the hand of God."

As he continued his travels, he began to feel that it was not his commission to organise a revival fellowship, but simply to preach and witness to his conviction concerning the needs and opportunities of the present hour in world history, and, especially, to endeavour to awaken people to prayer.

At the end of 1934, a young man called at the offices of Messrs. Marshall, Morgan and Scott with a manuscript which he wanted them to take. He would not be put off by any reference to the risk of publishing such a document from an unknown writer. In fact, he declared that it was the will of God that it should be published! The manuscript was the record of Edwin Orr's first journey. Within two years, the publishers tell us, a quarter of a million copies of this and subsequent books by this young man had been sold. They enjoyed a world-wide sale. This first of them was called *Can*

God——?, which, now in its fifteenth edition, provides the title for a condensation of the original book and the two which immediately followed it, giving accounts of further adventures on the Continent and in America and the Antipodes.

As he turned to still wider journeying, this first book obviously opened up the way for him.

Norway was the first foreign country visited, to which he travelled free by collier from Penarth Dock. When he arrived there he tells how a feeling of depression came over him, as he realised that he was in a foreign land, without friends, without food, without bed, and without the prospect of preaching, not knowing anything but a word or two of the language! Then, remembering a name once seen on a parcel in his publishers' office in England, he telephoned a certain Pastor Öhrn. A voice answered, and Edwin discovered that, that very morning, the man at the other end of the line had been reading his book, *Can God*——? Edwin Orr's travels in other lands had begun! He crashed into Finland, and even, in 1935, into Soviet Russia, practically impossible restrictions and difficulties being in some way resolved.

Travelling from Turkey to Greece, an astonishing thing happened which will stand as example of the nature of so many of Edwin Orr's adventures. The fare from Constantinople to Athens, so Cook's, the tourist agents, had informed him, was twelve Turkish pounds. Edwin had no money remaining, and the boat was to sail at nine in the morning. He had prayed about this matter, without telling anybody. At midnight on the night before, when saying goodbye to most of his Turkish friends, the passage-money still had not arrived. Without his knowledge, however, a "thank-offering" had been taken. It amounted to twenty-two pounds! When he went for his ticket to the purser's office on the boat, he was told that the information from Cook's was incorrect: the fare was not twelve pounds, but twenty-one and fifty piastres!

On this tour in which he travelled in thirty countries, every penny to make it possible, Orr tells us, was received from sources on the Continent itself: seventy per cent of these expenses reached him anonymously, passed on by being stuffed into his pocket, or enclosed with unsigned letters.

In 1935, Edwin Orr went to Canada and the United States, and in 1936 to New Zealand, Australia and South Africa. By now, he was taking part in mammoth evangelistic meetings. He was launched on a career that has continued in effectiveness.

In the war, he became a Chaplain in the U.S. Army Air Forces. Just before its outbreak, he had been doing a certain amount of academic work in Canada and the States. When his chaplaincy service ended, he returned to this country and attended Oxford University. In 1948 he received the Oxford degree of Doctor of Philosophy for his thesis, "The Second Evangelical Awakening in Britain".

This book describes an all-too-little regarded period in Britain, beginning in 1859, when the breath of revival swept through the land. With a total population in the country of only twenty-seven million it is impressive to realise that a million new members were added to the churches in those years. "Theatre services" were held to reach "outsiders", and 50,000 attended these in London alone. It was in those years that William Booth started on his career as an evangelist. It was a stirring time.

Behind this movement, so carefully analysed by Dr. Orr, there lay an initial prayer concern. The revival, indeed, went forward on a wave of prayer. Dr. Eugene Stock, for many years Secretary of the C.M.S., states in *My Recollections* that the revival in the years round 1860 was of a kind never experienced since in this country (excepting in the localized Welsh revival of 1905), its most striking feature being the phenomenon of the prayer-meeting. He pictures, for instance, the scene in the great hall at Islington, which he once saw packed from floor to ceiling with people who had come together for nothing else but prayer!

Behind Pentecost, Edwin Orr reminds us, was prayer. Behind the Moravian movement in Germany, reaching out across the world, was prayer. Prayer was implicit in the first Methodist awakening, and doubly was it behind the second great wave of "Primitive Methodism". It was the Fulton Street prayer-meeting in New York that started the 1859 revival, which spread across the whole of the English-speaking world. And it was prayer that was behind the Welsh revival of 1905. Small wonder that Edwin Orr, who has studied these things and been in the midst of evangelistic movements, states categorically that prayer is one of the necessary preconditions for revival.

It is interesting to note that in Glenn Clark's account of his "Prayer Journey" round the world, *On Wings of Prayer*,[1] Edwin Orr's name is mentioned. They met in Madras, where Dr. Orr was conducting an evangelistic meeting in the Memorial Hall. Of him Glenn Clark says this, "Edwin Orr is one of the clearest minds in Evangelism today, and because of his understanding and dedication can be a bridge to help bring religious leaders together in unity and goodwill—together around Jesus."

The picture we return to, however, is of the youthful Edwin, brash, impulsive, daring to start out on his crazy adventure, because he believes God is behind it, and God will see that he is supported. For us, he stands as an example of the spiritual adventurer, going forward in faith, trusting God implicitly, and looking to Him for the supply of all needs, physical, as well as spiritual.

In this he was obviously inspired by the kind of faith illustrated by the C.I.M. missionaries and such men and women as C. T. Studd and Amy Carmichael. Orr quotes with approval the words of Hudson Taylor, founder of the C.I.M.: "God's

[1] Published by Arthur James (Evesham).

work, done in God's way, will always be met by God's provision." He tells how on the flyleaf of the Bible which he had when he began his three-year tour of the world were the words of General Booth, "The Promises of God are sure—if you only believe", and underneath are the names of the forty-eight countries in which the note says, "Satisfactorily proved in——"

Surely there comes from this story an encouragement to a more daring, a more adventurous, faith. Most of us will be called to use this in other ways than the way Edwin Orr followed. Not necessarily shall we be called to leave our homes and start travelling round the world! But all of us can learn to pray the prayer of confidence and trust.

When Hudson Taylor first offered for missionary service in China, his friend, the local Congregational minister, asked him, "And how do you propose to go there?" "I answered," wrote Hudson Taylor, "that I did not know; it seemed probable that I should need to do as the Twelve and the Seventy in Judea, who went without purse or script, relying on Him who sent me to supply all my need." The minister placed his hand on young Hudson Taylor's shoulder in a kindly manner, and said, "Ah, my boy, as you grow older you will become wiser than that. Such an idea would do very well in the days when Christ Himself was on earth, but not now."

Many years afterwards, recalling this, the veteran missionary added, "I have grown older since then, but not wiser. I am more and more convinced that if we were to take the directions of our Master, and the assurance He gave to His first disciples, more fully as our guide, we should find them just as suited to our times as to those in which they were originally given."

With his bicycle and two shillings and eightpence farthing, Edwin Orr so found it, when in 1933 he started on his journey. He knew little more of the future than that he intended to do what he felt the Lord wanted him to do. It was an adventure of faith.

EXPLORERS IN PRAYER

3. STANLEY JONES

Apart from me you can do nothing.

1098495<small>JOHN 15: 5</small>

IN MARCH 1958, a missionary was travelling on the mail train from Sealdah to Siliguri, in India. Between Katihsa Junction (which was reached about twelve o'clock midnight) and Islampur Station (which the train would pass at about 3 a.m.) he was robbed and thrown out on the line, to be discovered, bleeding and unconscious, at seven o'clock next morning by a Mr. Kundu of Islampur, an Indian Roman Catholic.

The man's condition was so terrible that he was completely unrecognizable. The Bengali doctor in the Siliguri Hospital, to which he was taken immediately, reported his condition as "very critical", with multiple head injuries, cuts and bruises all over his face and other parts of his body. Police enquiries had already begun to establish his identity. His name was Stanley Jones. In this critical condition he was moved to Calcutta, where X-ray examination revealed a skull fracture, a large intra-cranial haemorrhage and a post-orbital clot producing pressure on the optic nerve. Three days after the event, the doctor in charge of his case said, "He is just with us" and when asked about sending for his wife in England commented, "It may be too late, but the sooner she is here the better".

35

All denominations and all races and folk of all religions prayed for him. Gradually Stanley Jones began to mount the hill towards recovery. He has since been home on furlough, and hopes to be in full service again. "There is no doubt that the fact that he is alive is a miracle," says one report concerning him. "God has answered the prayers of many people, in England, in Bengal, and throughout India."

I have seen a copy of a letter sent by his wife, Alison, in which she expresses thanks to all those who helped so splendidly. She says that she is grateful most of all for the continued prayers "from Christian communities everywhere . . . it was this that kept us going and helped us through those very difficult days. I have said Christian communities," she continues, "but I am too narrow in that because we had word from some of the Christians in Sarenga, some of our old servants and friends, saying 'Will you please tell the Mem Saheb that even the non-Christians are praying for the Saheb's recovery and for her and the children.'"

When I first heard this story my mind immediately flew to thinking of Stanley Jones, the veteran missionary, internationally famous, who is an American Methodist. But the Stanley Jones in question, I soon discovered, is the Rev. A. Stanley Jones, B.A., not the Rev. Dr. E. Stanley Jones. More than that, I realised that I knew him: for one year, when he was in his first year and I in my fourth, A. Stanley Jones and I were colleagues in College!

The confusion of names led me to further thinking about E. Stanley Jones, and to a re-appraisal of his significant contribution to prayer-discovery. The mistake that I made for a little while was one easy to make, for the story was one exactly suited. Prayer, other people's sustaining prayer, has meant much to him, as it has meant to his namesake. And if anything of the nature of the train attack had happened to him there would have been, without any question, a volume of prayer going up from all over the world, from Christian and non-Christian alike.

Dr. E. Stanley Jones is a man who has led a remarkable life. It was in 1907 that he went to India as a missionary, spending much of his endeavour in winning educated high-caste Indians for Christ. In 1924 he wrote the book which made his international reputation, *The Christ of the Indian Road*. It was the first of many books which have been universally read and translated into many languages. In his work as evangelist and as one seeking to lead people to experiment in prayer and to venture further in spiritual things, he has used with great advantage, both in India and America, a method which is an adaptation of an Indian idea: that of the Ashram, a sort of "Camp Farthest Out", where folk live, work, play and worship together in circumstances of great intimacy and fellowship.

Concerning the power behind this full life of his he says, "If there is a secret, it is in these two things: I have kept my prayer life intact, and I've always had tasks I couldn't do." Thrown back on God, he has learned to depend on Him for adequacy. Stanley Jones is never tired of reiterating that there are two great laws of life, which work implicitly in everything to do with prayer: on the one hand, receptivity, and on the other, response and creativity.

Prayer, he says, is co-operation with God, attunement with Him and His purposes, penetration into the spiritual realm; or, putting it another way, it is "receptivity to reality" and "response to God". He quotes from the original *Reader's Digest* article on *Prayer* from which Alexis Carrel's book on Prayer was expanded, in which the Doctor says that "prayer is the most powerful form of energy one can generate": it is this, says Stanley Jones, because it is receiving from God. To know how to receive is life's most important lesson. "Jesus

37

trained His followers for three years in one thing and only one thing—receptivity."

In his book, *Mastery*, he develops the theme that in the Book of Acts we have an account of the cleanest, sanest, wisest and most powerful use of prayer ever recorded. Here were men who had seen prayer at work in the life of Jesus; and who, at his instigation, started as a group praying for one thing—the Holy Spirit (Acts 1: 14). To this unconditional praying, God gave the answer (Acts 2: 4). The Book goes on to show these men, under the guidance and power of the Spirit, continuing in this line of praying that is always answered. It is the kind of praying that Stanley Jones covets for himself and others.

It is in terms of personal experience that he knows so much about it. "I do not argue the question as to whether anything happens in prayer," he writes in *The Christ of Every Road*—"I simply testify: it does!" For years, he tells us, "I have lived on power not my own. . . . On arrival in India I was told that I would break down within a year if I kept up the pace at which I was going. This would have been true had there not been the rejuvenation that comes from the fellowship of the Spirit." In *Abundant Living* he writes, "I have lived for 35 years in one of the worst climates in the world—India, a land poverty-stricken and disease-ridden, 'the white man's grave'. And yet I have come out of it (1945) at the end of these years with a better body than when I went in. I have missed only about two single engagements in 25 years: one from a flu germ—the gift of America—and one by a war regulation in Ceylon."

The fact is that at the beginning of his ministry in India he started in at such a pace that it seemed impossible that he could keep going. After a few months he came to the point of complete physical and mental exhaustion. One night, as he finished an address, he knew that he could not go on; but, as he moved away from the platform, these words sounded in his soul, "Why don't you let me take over?" Why not? Overwhelmingly and utterly, he answered, "Do Lord, completely, now". Describing what happened afterwards he said, "It seemed as though I walked on air that night". He had found the secret of receiving power—the kind of "surrender" to God, which means that, letting him "take over", there are now no barriers to the inflow of His grace and power.

That "healing"—for it most certainly was that—says Dr. Jones, was "apparently functional". Following this report on himself which we have quoted above, made in 1945, he now tells us that he received another healing, this one "apparently structural". He was about to go on an evangelistic tour round the world. The routine mission-board check-up revealed that he "had sugar". The specialist reported, "You have a mildly serious case of diabetes. It won't get any better—it will probably get worse, and it will hasten your deterioration." Since Stanley Jones "pays his own way" and is independent of the mission board, he went on this tour notwithstanding. "You go," was what he says he heard the Father say to him. "In Me you are well and whole. And there will be a minimum of strain with a maximum of result." The diabetes cleared progressively and he spoke from two to five times a day for three months of ceaseless travel, during which time 36,000 people signed "decision cards".

Stanley Jones is very fond of quoting the story of a missionary friend who was about to leave India, discouraged and broken, when he discovered the verses in John 4: 13ff, and took hold of what is promised there. "Drinks and keeps on drinking" was how he came to read the meaning of the verb (it is in the "continuous present" in the Greek): "whosoever drinketh of the water that I shall give him shall never thirst." Years later this man, now transformed—a man whose influence is now world-wide—said, "Since that time 35 years ago, I have not had a single dark, discouraged hour". I have often wondered whether this "missionary friend" to whom he so often refers may not have had the initials E.S.J.

"Receiving," after this fashion, is only possible when, from our side, there are no barriers, when we are prepared to live by Him and for Him. On our side of this experience there must be what Stanley Jones speaks of as "surrender". He regards this as the initial secret of the Christian life and the key to prayer. It was so in his own case: "I laid at his feet," he tells us, "a self of which I was ashamed, couldn't control and couldn't live with; and to my glad astonishment He took that self, remade it, consecrated it to Kingdom purposes, gave it back to me, a self I can now live with gladly and joyously and comfortably." In this way, at a later stage, through a renewal of this consecration of his "all", he knew the coming of the Spirit's power in a deeper fullness.

This kind of praying is not self-centred. In it we are not asking for God's spiritual gifts merely for ourselves. It is not, as Stanley Jones describes it, an "ego-expanding cult". We are not using God. We surrender to Him and His purposes. Any new sense of power and reality which He gives us but fits us the better to serve Him. We are not bending God to our will, but "blending our wills with His". "Through prayer, we begin to live by His power."

Prayer then, says Stanley Jones, is "fundamentally and essentially self-surrender". Once he asked Kagawa what he thought was the first thing in prayer, and the great Japanese Christian answered with this one word, "Surrender". It is not mere submission, passivity, that is asked for: "Prayer is the wire surrendering to the dynamo, the flower surrendering to the sun, the child surrendering to education, the patient surrendering to the surgeon, the part surrendering to the whole —prayer is life surrendering to Life."

By giving up the self completely to God, one is "getting

self out of the way"; and the surrender makes possible the receiving of all that God wishes to give, and a free response to all that He asks. Continually renewed, and made specially definite at certain times, "surrender" of this order is the key to prayer—the kind of praying that is answered.

4. GLENN CLARK

THE PRAYER OF RELINQUISHMENT

In all thy ways acknowledge him, and he shall direct thy paths.
PROVERBS 3: 6

IT IS a thrilling and astonishing thing that a layman, professor
of English in an American university college, and coach,
over many years, to its athletics team, should have seen the
vision of a widening movement built up with the one object of
fostering prayer, and should have seen that movement grow,
and, before his life ended, should have undertaken a "Prayer
Journey" through Britain, Holland, Germany, Italy, Greece,
Egypt, Jordan, the Lebanon, Syria, Iraq, Pakistan, India,
Ceylon, Malaya, Thailand, Hongkong, the Philippines,
Formosa, Okinawa, Japan, Wake, Hawaii, and back to the
United States!

In 1939 this man, Dr. Glenn Clark, with a group of friends,
launched a "three-year plan". He caught the imagination of
increasing numbers of like-minded people as the movement
gathered momentum. Already known to many, through his
books and pamphlets, he was enabled, through the help of an
American trust known as the *Louise Memorial Foundation*, to
send out his appeal and to establish a magazine called *Clear
Horizons*, which would foster it. It was all part of a concern he
had had for years: to introduce people to the power of prayer,
and especially to mobilise prayer in the face of the threat to
peace which has been so repeatedly before this generation.

He likened prayer, in this modern situation, to the "sling-shot of David". In place of the confidence that others put in armies, battleships and machine-guns, he desired to see confidence springing to birth in God's power, known through prayer. How utterly inadequate the youthful David must have looked as he went out to encounter Goliath! How foolish, with no weapon and no armour save his sling and the five smooth stones out of the brook! Yet he won. The Lord was with him.

Glenn Clark's call in 1939 was for three hundred volunteers to form a sort of "Gideon's Band" of people proving God by their courage and their faith in prayer. The response far exceeded his initial hopes. And what has widened from it is far more important than any organisation. Through the magazine, through his *Camps Farthest Out*, and through the extended publicity given to his books, many have been encouraged to experiment in prayer, and to match the modern giants of materialism, despotism and sin with this "sling-shot of David".

Perhaps Glenn Clark's most interesting, and most colourful, venture, has been his founding of the *Camps Farthest Out*. Readers will doubtless already have detected a certain literary flamboyance and imaginative venturing in the kind of titles that Glenn Clark gave to his ideas. He was a "literary" man, given to the encouragement of people's imaginative and creative gifts.

He began his career, after receiving his M.A. from Harvard in 1908, as a high-school principal, and then became a college professor, for twenty years of that time acting as coach for the athletes of Macalester, Minnesota, with the greatest of success in that last capacity by the way! As a result of his own spiritual experience, he began to write his books and pamphlets, and came to be in great demand as a lecturer at student conventions, business-men's organisations, as well as in the churches, and at retreats for the churches' leaders.

In the early nineteen-twenties, he happened to visit Monhegan Island, off the Coast of Maine, known as the "Island Farthest Out". What a wonderful thing, he thought, if, say, a hundred people could come to a place like this for a week, "together learning how to fall into balance, physically, mentally, and spiritually so completely that they could stay in balance all year".

The invitation went out, and the first Camp was held at Lake Koronis, in Minnesota. The name itself proved a point of interest from the start, and Dr. Clark improved upon the leverage into minds that it offered by pointing to the "Realm Farthest Out"—beyond the material and the intellectual—into which its spiritual adventurers were invited to explore.

People who have been to the Camps say that they afford an experience totally unlike any other that has come to them. In the first place, they have to learn how to "unbend"—literally as well as metaphorically! The "exercises in creative motion" are something which staid middle-aged people find more than a little unusual. One of Glenn Clark's favourite slogans has been "Let go and let God". It is only as we get ourselves out of the way that God can pour what He will into us, and through us into the life of the world. The spirit of partnership with Christ and oneness with each other is in itself stimulated by sharing in things which break down one's pride and our isolating sophistication.

The actual sessions of the first days of the Camps are spent in "prayer laboratories", in which all are encouraged to test and prove, to seek and find. Those who speak at the sessions, as Dr. Clark himself expresses it, "are people who have gone farthest out in surrendering their lives to Christ. They don't talk of and about the Kingdom of Heaven, they immerse their listeners in it". A good deal of time is spent in creative work and sharing together—music, painting and writing. After the first sessions the Camp is broken up into smaller Prayer Cells

44

of some ten or twelve, who remain together in prayer endeavour for the rest of the week, while lectures, discussions and prayer hours for all clarify underlying principles.

This is the kind of thing that one might find oneself sharing in—and never forgetting afterwards!—a "Broadcast of Love to all the world". Assembling after their evening meal, the campers, holding candles symbolising the love of God shining in a dark world, are formed into three great circles. The symbolism of the circles Glenn Clark interprets as representing our concern, our love, our prayer, in the One Church of Light engirdling the world. Together, as we hold out our arms, or lift them over our heads, consciously and actively we broadcast our love, turning to the four points of the compass as we do so. And we take our circle, in turn, to the great focal centres of the world—London, Washington, Delhi, Peking, Moscow, and pray for people and leaders as we surround them in love.

"I believe," Dr. Clark once wrote, "that if a sufficient number of people would draw apart awhile in retreats or camps and study and practise the art of prayer for an adequate period of time in this letting-go fashion, the problems of the world would be solved better and quicker than by any other known method. If corporate prayer continued long enough, wars and the causes of war would soon cease."

It was conviction of this kind that sent Glenn Clark on his mission of prayer round the world in January 1954, a mission which he himself described in *On Wings of Prayer*. In some of the most unexpected places Glenn Clark and Roland and Marcia Brown, who accompanied him, not only spoke to groups, large and small, but also formed some of these groups into a "Camp Farthest Out"; so that "two hundred and thirty sturdy Britons" at Swanwick, two groups of young people in Holland (Queen Juliana, by the way, was most interested to learn about the Camps and their methods!), and a group of missionaries and Indians at Nasrapur, had an introduction to

45

them. After sharing in this latter Camp, the Y.M.C.A. Secretary of Poona said, "This camp must be perpetuated . . . Many churches are spiritually dead, many Y.M.C.A.'s are just marking time; this type of camp can put new life into the dead bones of India's Christianity."

Glenn Clark has told[1] how he grew up in a family circle full of the spirit of love and self-forgetfulness. When there came the first break in that loved circle, the experience was so difficult and bewildering that for a whole year he seemed to be stumbling and groping after faith. One day the words "Acknowledge Him in all your ways and He will direct thy paths" impressed themselves on his mind with great force. Something within him leapt to answer. It was a real moment of surrender, and the burden of running his own life and worrying about its problems fell from him. For a month thereafter, life was triumph and bliss. Then the experience faded, self became dominant and obtrusive again; and not until some years later did he find his way back, permanently, to the same attitude of heart and mind. The secret, he discovered, lay in finding the right way to pray.

It almost seemed as if his new method was something he had stumbled on by himself—until he realised that he was using the method of the Lord's Prayer. It is Glenn Clark's belief that that prayer is meant to be a frame on which to build our thoughts and meditations. The first part prepares us for communion, and it is that, says he, that is by far "the bigger half" of prayer! We put ourselves in tune with God; then we ask Him to open His Kingdom of power and love to us and express it through us, and then we lose our troubles and our needs in this divine stream. We are channels for God's Love. Our prayer helps us so to be.

It is in his book, *Healing through Prayer* that he tells us

[1] In a booklet entitled *The Lord's Prayer and other talks on Prayer* (originally given, by the way, at "Camps Farthest Out").

about "the prayer of relinquishment". We should like, in this chapter, to isolate this as his special contribution to the principles we are looking at together. It enables us to understand a great deal concerning the secrets of answered prayer.

This kind of praying is, in effect, the working out of the phrase so often used in prayer: "if it be Thy will". The phrase, however, is often used in a negative fashion that has the effect of cancelling out the request that we have just made. We pray (in faith?) for someone's recovery, and, since we think it right, and our duty, since Christ prayed this prayer himself in Gethsemane,[1] we add (in doubt?), "if it be Thy will". The certainty that faith requires is at variance with the doubt we have ourselves introduced. Not so with the prayer of relinquishment. We have given ourselves over, gladly and absolutely to God. And now we give the person for whom we are praying to Him. We are surrendering our own possessiveness.

In many a baptismal service for infant children these words are used, "You are come here to acknowledge that this, your child, belongs to God, and to receive him again as from the hands of God to be trained as a disciple of our Lord and Saviour Jesus Christ." The fact however is, if we are honest, that those hands that receive the little one back again are hands which all too often proclaim that he is "our child" much more than that "he belongs to God". The prayer of relinquishment

[1] We must remember the special circumstances under which Christ first used this petition, in Gethsemane. The circumstances are completely unparalleled in any prayer that we shall ever have to offer. He knew that His mission was to *deal* with man's sin, and for long past He had known that the way led to the Cross. Now that the time was come, He realised how dark and black was the way immediately ahead—and how it involved the complete unmasking of sin where ordinarily it remains hidden—one of his disciples was to betray Him, another to deny Him, leaders and people were to show themselves in the very worst light. Is there any other way?— that is the point of the prayer. *And when Christ knows that there is not*— note this—He now unhesitatingly goes forward *in faith*. He merges His human will and understanding with the Will of the Father.

47

really lets him go. It is something some of us learn only after a long time.

Once, so Glenn Clark tells us, he was asked to pray for a little Catholic boy, apparently dying from spinal meningitis. The parents were holding on to him, fighting for his life. Dr. Clark tells us that he felt that his prayers were "hitting the ceiling"—a ceiling created by the parents' own wills. Then there came the report to him, "The boy is scarcely breathing. The priest has administered Extreme Unction." "Then his parents have given him up completely at last?" "Yes, they are reconciled now to what is to happen. It is God's will, they say, and they have given him up to the Father." "Good," replied Glenn Clark. "Now we can roll up our sleeves and start in to pray." And they did! Now there was no "ceiling" holding down their prayers. Within a few days, the child was well.

There came a time when Dr. Clark's own children, two girls, aged fourteen and twelve, were both desperately ill with scarlet fever. Their throats were contracted to such an extent that not even a drop of water could pass. Breathing was only just possible. When the doctor sent for the ambulance, he said, "I lost a patient last week whose condition was much less serious than this."

"You've often told others they must relinquish their children to the Father," said his wife to him. "Now is the time when we must relinquish ours. If it is God's Plan for them to go, rather than that they should be crippled, or weakened all their lives by this illness, I would be willing that God should take them. We know that we alone would suffer—for them it would be a great and glorious experience."

"I have just this one prayer to offer for their recovery," added Glenn, "it is this: That if they are to enter the Kingdom, we promise here that we shall try to make our home so complete an expression of the Kingdom of Heaven on earth that, if God wishes them to abide in the Kingdom, He may let them abide in our home instead."

The father adds this to his account of what happened, "When a few weeks later the little girls were restored to us, with no after effects of the illness at all, completely recovered, their eyes seemed to shine with the light of heaven within them."

"I have found," says Glenn Clark, "that it is not the prayer that creates the miracle, but the condition in consciousness that the prayer induces." We can see what happens, thus, when we pray the "prayer of relinquishment"—one more barrier is down that has kept the love and power of God at bay. Our love for our own loved one is no longer possessive. We have surrendered him or her into the loving hands of the Father. What we want for our loved one is the loving Will of Him Who knows, as we do not, what really is best.

When we let our loved ones go, like that, something has gone in us which was a barrier to the full flowing of God's love and power into the whole situation—into us, and through us, to the loved ones. The answering power is no longer impeded by the barrier of possessiveness on our side.

5. MURIEL LESTER

The Prayer of Relaxation

Be still, and know that I am God.

PSALM 46: 10

MURIEL LESTER is a fighter and not least a fighter in the cause of pacifism. It is therefore not a little amusing that the particular facet of prayer which we shall be introducing under her name has to do with that blessed word "relaxation". Amusing, perhaps, but very instructive! Not a little of the drive and energy that she is still able to display, dashing about the world in the name of one good cause or another at the age of 74, is due, she would tell you, to the lesson she once learned about God the Source of Power being available to all, through prayer.

But let us begin with a few facts about her. In early childhood (as she tells us in her fascinating autobiography, *It Occurred to Me*) she was a "militarist patriot". Lord Roberts, Lord Kitchener and the rest were her heroes, and throughout the Boer War her mind was set on the righteousness of our cause. After going away to school at St. Andrews in Scotland, she settled down happily in her very comfortable and beautiful home in Loughton, Essex. This did not mean staying at home, for her mother and father loved travelling and they spent most winters in Italy and France. Once they went to Palestine.

It was an invitation to a Christmas party at a factory girl's club which took her down to Bow for the first time. Up till then she had only known the East End of London as a horrid smelly place to hurry through. It was thought of as "the disreputable haunt of thieves, drunks and hooligans". Meeting these girls as her hostesses introduced Muriel to the real East End. They seemed to her ignorance a new kind of people and she longed to know them better. She promptly joined the club and soon delighted in the pluck and good humour of the workers.

Muriel's younger sister, Doris, had also become interested in Bow folk and she began, what Muriel soon came to follow, the habit of living in Bow for periods at a time. Their brother Kingsley soon joined them and they rented a house there, had it deloused and re-papered and started housekeeping together. One or other of the sisters was always at home with their beloved parents at Loughton. A topic often discussed at interdenominational conferences of that era was "How to reach the masses". Going to live with them seemed to the young Lesters the simplest expedient.

Just at the outset of the 1914-18 war, Kingsley, the beloved brother, died at the early age of twenty-six. In lieu of a will, he had left a sheet of notepaper outlining a few gifts, and leaving the rest of the money "to Muriel and Doris that the income from it may be used in their work among the people of Bow or wherever else they may go". Then as a living memorial to him their father offered to purchase premises in Bow where they could set up what they had so often planned together, a sort of "teetotal pub", a place where all could find fellowship, high and low, rich and poor, enemy, neutral and ally, protestant, catholic and atheist. So Kingsley Hall began, with as little defined policy as that. Through the years it has continued to serve the people of Bow in countless ways and over the years has become more and more defined as a place of worship round which social activities and facilities are grouped.

Mary Hughes of Whitechapel—daughter of the author of *Tom Brown's School Days*—came to live at Kingsley Hall and to help in the work. In Muriel Lester's book *Praying; How, When, Where, and Why*[1] there is an unforgettable picture of Mary Hughes in those days of 1915.

"I begged her one bitter cold day to let me light the gas-heater installed against her will in her bedroom. 'But, I don't notice the cold,' she declared. 'Feel my hands, dear. You see? I'm always burning with indignation at the way we let the poor suffer.'" It was true; her hands were much warmer than Muriel's who says that she found this an illustration of an axiom which Mary Hughes lived by. "Whether you are ill or well depends on how many seconds of the twenty-four hours you think about God."

Shortly after leaving school Muriel discovered Tolstoy's book, *The Kingdom of God is Within You*. It was this that irrevocably "tipped me right over into pacifism, a swift transition for such an absurdly militarist young woman, but once your eyes get opened to Christian pacifism, you can't shut them again. Once you see it, you can't unsee it".

Doubtless this new uncompromising attitude added to the difficulties inherent in starting such a place as Kingsley Hall. Upholding pacifist principles during war, organising the growing work of the Hall, dealing with its human problems, became difficult when Mr. Lester was taken seriously ill: Muriel had to go home. On returning to Bow again, her heart began to behave badly. For eight months she struggled to get better but as soon as she got stronger and felt the least bit fitter, even the mildest excitement allowed by her doctor— a tea-party or a visitor—sent her right back again.

It was a comment made by her masseuse that at length started her on the path of discovery. It startled and challenged her. In *Ways of Praying* Muriel tells the story, how twice a week the masseuse came to "pummel her", and one day quietly announced, "You don't seem able ever to get well. It's your temperament. You enjoy everything too much."

[1] Published by the Independent Press.

This remark sent Muriel searching into herself and into the nature of God's ways with us human beings.

It was a dull November day when this bombshell—for such was its effect—burst. She walked up and down the moss-grown paths in the damp garden; the day seemed exactly to match her mood. "I felt as though I was wandering about on the floor of hell and as the darkness engulfed me, I knew only one thing: that there could be no respite from struggle until I had somehow discovered how to harness my own puny, unreliable spirit to the Eternal Spirit."

She had to make an intense effort but the centre of it, oddly enough, was to practise the prayer of relaxation.

She says, "I had been physically strung-up like a bit of over-stretched elastic: like yesterday's lettuce in a house where there's no Frigidaire: jerky like a gramophone when the record's got broken or the needle worn down."

For an hour a day she forced herself to lie on her back in an upstairs bedroom and remember God. She encouraged her breathing to get slower, deeper, more rhythmical, reminding herself that with each breath she drew she was actually taking in something of the breath of God. She would match the Genesis affirmation with the rhythm of her breathing: "He breathed into man's nostrils the breath of life and man became a living soul" (Genesis 2:7.) She reminded herself that "breathe" is the Anglo-Saxon form of the latinized word, "Spirit".

It sometimes took twelve or fourteen minutes of this sort of praying before the tense muscles completely relaxed— before hands, toes, lips, forehead stopped tightening up again, and again. When at last the necessary relaxation was achieved the rest of the hour was spent in linking others in her mind to this immense source of Peace and Joy and Power.

After keeping at this for a month she presented herself to the local doctor and her heart was pronounced excellent, adequate to anything. From then on she knew how to take the strain, how to let it go. Says she, "I felt that prayer was like a good, strong raft on which men could ride over the deepest and blackest of waters in safety and delight." It was a discovery indeed.

No one since has been busier nor more involved in problems near and far. A month or so after its foundation Muriel Lester identified herself with the work of the Fellowship of Reconciliation and attended the Conference in 1920 where Christian pacifists from various countries came together to form the International Fellowship of Reconciliation. Local affairs at Bow claimed most of her time and for four and a half years, in company with George Lansbury, she served on the Poplar Borough Council as Alderman. One would need a long list to catalogue all the work she has done and the causes with which she has been associated.

In 1926 she stayed for a month with Mahatma Gandhi at his Ashram in India. She asked him to come to England. He outlined his conditions, "I will come if you rouse public opinion, stir up the churches, get hold of Members of Parliament and convince Cabinet Ministers that what you have seen here as regards your Government's drink and opium policy is thwarting India's passion for the prohibition of these two evils." She was given instructions how to collect and check information about these things before leaving India. She was to go to the Governors of Bengal and Bombay, also to the Viceroy, telling them what she intended reporting on her return home. Then she must see the Secretary of State for India in London, Lord Birkenhead. "Why do you shrink?" Gandhi asked when she said that she could not bring herself to do this last thing. "The worst they can do is to refuse to help you. In that case you must turn their refusal into your strength."

On her return Muriel wrote a book, *My Host the Hindu*. It was followed very soon by another entitled *Entertaining Gandhi* for when the great Indian Leader came over for the Round Table Conference in 1931, he stayed the whole ten weeks at Kingsley Hall among the people of Bow. When pressed by West End friends to stay just one night with them, he answered "No, here I am doing the real Round Table Conference work, getting to know the people of England".

In 1935 she went to China to investigate a charge that had been brought to her notice concerning the Japanese militarists' illegal traffic in poisonous drugs. The drug pedlars were usually Formosans or Koreans, who were spreading this prohibited trade under "Extra-territorial rights" over most of China. When she faced an influential Japanese in Tokyo, endeavouring to elicit his help in beginning her investigation, she followed Gandhi's way of "truth telling" and confessed to the same sort of sins which her own country had committed against the Chinese in the Opium Wars of the last century. Hers was a dangerous mission. After it was over, she went back to Tokyo, giving her report first to one statesman, one minister, then another. She then was invited to Geneva to report to the Chairman of the League of Nations Opium Committee. By this time she had given up leadership of Kingsley Hall and had become the Travelling Secretary of the Fellowship of Reconciliation. She has just completed her ninth journey round the world.

We have recorded enough of this busy woman's life to make it clear that the "prayer of relaxation" is something recommended by a person who has been in the frontline of social endeavour and has campaigned for social justice on half a dozen fronts.

She has suffered obloquy and misunderstanding countless times, but has fought undeterred in her campaign for the Kingdom of God to be set up on earth. Nor has she been exempt, in all this, from the lowly, practical service of the "foot washing".

55

All that she has to say about prayer is of the greatest value, but we, in this chapter isolate, as her special contribution, this suggestion, which is so full of value to the over-tense, the preternaturally tired, concerning the association of deep, complete physical relaxation with the spirit of prayer: letting things go, relying on God's Presence, breathing in His great gifts of Peace and Joy and Energy.

"Be still and know that I am God," says the Psalmist in verse 1c of Psalm 46. God is the Source of Life. Through prayer, and particularly through this kind of praying, we make contact with Him and are revived at our centre, recreated. "Underneath are the everlasting arms." "Casting all your care upon Him for he careth for you." These are not just sentences with a beautifully comforting sound. They enshrine some of life's deepest truths. If we can learn to "let go, and let God", we shall find something of the answer, a form of praying that not only enabled Muriel Lester to overcome an illness that looked like staying with her for the rest of her life, but enabled her to do far more, afterwards, than she was doing before. This is a form of "giving up" that the busiest of us would do very well to learn. In it is the secret of a "rest" from which one rises rejuvenated, re-equipped.

*Forgive, if ye have aught against any: that your Father also
which is in heaven may forgive you your trespasses.*

MARK 11: 25

THERE IS an important passage in Matthew, chapter 6.
Jesus is speaking of prayer. After giving the model prayer,
He goes on to mention one of the great barriers that men set
between themselves and God which prevents any real answer
coming to them. He thus doubly emphasises its importance,
because "forgive us our debts, as we forgive our debtors" is
embedded in the very heart of the model prayer, and now He
comments, "If you forgive not men their trespasses, neither
will your Father forgive your trespasses." It was an experience which involved the full working out of this principle
that proved to be pivotal and crucial in the life of Florence
Allshorn. It aided her in her future work in training others,
and made her see the front-rank importance of right relationships, in connection with all Christian work. It also liberated
her to a fullness of service and a quality of Christian leadership of outstanding character and value.

Florence was orphaned while quite young, and was brought
up by an unmarried relative in an unloving environment and
in a dreary house in Sheffield. After day school, and a course
in the School of Art, which was unfortunately abbreviated
because of oncoming eye strain, she studied for four years at

57

the Sheffield School of Domestic Science. This double training, she always said, taught her to look at things, to discern their real qualities, and it enabled her to develop her creative gifts in a practical way.

Beginning to be drawn into the activities of Sheffield Cathedral, and into the friendship of those at the centre of its life, she herself became the inspirational, vivacious leader of a club for factory girls, a teacher in the Sunday School, and eventually a full-time member of the staff. It was in 1920 that she offered for missionary service, and was sent, under the Church Missionary Society, to Iganga in Busoga; and it was here that what we regard as the crucial experience in her growing Christianity came to her.

Travellers speak of this district in Uganda as a singularly depressing place. The climate itself saps soul and body. Some have confessed to a "psychic pressure of evil" uniquely felt in this area, as if some brooding evil cast a subtle shadow over it. Be that as it may, Florence followed seven other young missionaries who had come to Iganga, none of whom stayed longer than a year. The trouble was not only the climate and the intangible spirit of evil of the place, but the temperament of the senior woman missionary. It may help to suggest what this was by revealing that, when Florence arrived, she found the one and only sitting-room divided into two halves. Her colleague's furniture was crowded into one section. Pointing to the empty space, the other said, "That's your half."

In an article written much later in the *International Review of Missions*, Florence reveals the peculiar difficulties of women missionaries, and describes how some, compensating for an inner failure in their emotional life, fall victim to an inordinate craving for success in "the job" One has seen this "compensation" at work. It manifests itself, as Florence Allshorn declares, in "an urgent desire for power", and involves a loss of normal womanly quality, as well as of Christ-likeness and

58

humility. No doubt something of this kind could be diagnosed of the "difficult colleague" in Uganda, who also, it must not be forgotten, had had to spend years in this oppressive spot.

"Do pray God to keep near me and to keep me gentle and loving in my thoughts," Florence wrote to one of her friends. J. H. Oldham, in his book on Florence Allshorn, tells of an occasion when this difficult colleague was "in one of her furious tempers. She had hurled at Florence bitter and hurtful words. Florence remained silent. 'O God,' she prayed inwardly, 'help me to be sorry—to love her.' She clung desperately to the thought of God's infinite pity. Suddenly the angry words ceased, and the older woman said, 'You will never know what you have done for me,' and went quietly to her own room."

Thus were the victories won. The event that affected Florence most, and made her pray for an overcoming spirit of love in this desperate situation, was when the African matron said to her, "I've been on this station for fifteen years, and I have seen you come out, all of you, saying you have brought to us a Saviour, but I have never seen this situation saved yet."

What happens when love comes into a situation is that victories are won on all sides of the relationship. Something melts within one person—and then within the other person, too. It was so here. "Both of us," said Florence, "found our way to lighten each other. She had a great generosity and I must have been a cruel burden to her, worn out as she was. But I did see that as we two drew together in a new relation the whole character of the work on the station altered."

In her account, Florence is very anxious to decry the rôle of "the great reconciler". What happened, she said, was that her older colleague "had been beaten in that place, and I was only in the process of being beaten, and the old matron saved me". The latter's remark did more than that. It brought love right into the heart of the situation, releasing Florence from a dangerous and deepening preoccupation with herself. For the next year, she tells us, 1 Corinthians 13 became her daily reading. She needed this reminder and this reinforcement, every day. She was learning how to accept her colleague, and to love her just as she was. "What everything needs here," she wrote in a letter, "is to be deluged in love: *everything* wants loving." She had found that Love (Christian *agapē*) is the key to the most hopeless situation.

It is not surprising, as J. H. Oldham tells us, that, later, when some of her students wrote to her, reporting that they were facing very difficult conditions, Florence would often reply— doubtless to the amazement of the recipient—"Good, this is your chance, don't miss it."

Instead of the one year that had been the limit of her seven predecessors, Florence stayed for four years at the mission school at Iganga. She met with much success. Many girls, naturally lethargic and indolent, discovered a new quality of living altogether under her influence. "Busoga is a country that pulls at the heart-strings," was her final assessment. "Only the power of God is sufficient for it."

Those years, however, had taken their toll physically. After some months at home she was found to be in an advanced stage of tuberculosis. The specialist advised an operation, and told her that she might not live for more than two years! This operation was never performed, and she lived for twenty-five well-filled years thereafter. It was at this time that the Rev. John Maillard, that passionate crusader for Christian healing, helped her. She came to believe that God answers the prayer of faith regarding sickness and illness, and that it was not His will that her body should be under par. He still had work ahead for her to do.

There is a passage in her *Notebooks*,[1] in which she says,

---

[1] *The Notebooks of Florence Allshorn* selected and arranged by a member of St. Julian's Community (S.C.M. 1957).

"faith is not an easy thing to come by". So much has she learned from her experiences that she continues, "You are fortunate if you have been ill enough to think that only faith will save you. Then you have to have it." In another passage, she declares her own belief when she writes, "When I pray for the sick in body or soul, I imagine that person as God meant him to be, restored, whole, triumphant with health and vitality." For Florence to think so of herself, at this time, needed the greatest effort of faith and imagination. The fight was on! Sickness was the enemy, but with God were all the forces of life and the very power to inspire us to faith and to enable us to hold to it, and to increase it in us. Gradually, she won through, especially after the winter, spent in a sanatorium in Switzerland. The further year of "rest" that was ordered took her to a happy-go-lucky community run by "an enterprising woman" near Storrington, Sussex. Lessons learned there, in the give and take of human relationships amidst a very mixed group of some thirty people, stood her in good stead later.

In 1928 she was asked to undertake the wardenship of a Training College for C.M.S. women missionaries. At the beginning the appointment was purely temporary, but it lasted, finally, for eleven years. To this work, Florence brought the knowledge gained in her own experience, and she began a quiet revolution in the methods of training missionaries. Her realisation was that the most important area of a woman's life was largely being overlooked in the older methods of training. Unless the missionary's own emotional life had been stabilised, failure on the mission field was almost inevitable: and it would almost certainly be failure in demonstrating the power of the Gospel to affect human relationships—which, in itself, is something which strikes at the root of effective Christian witness. "We shall have to realize," she wrote, "that in building up the recruit, the mental and emotional health is of even more importance than the health of the body." The kind of deliverance Florence hoped to see in her students, since she knew at first-hand the importance of it, was that from preoccupation with self.

She saw, too, the importance of allowing a missionary a breathing-space and time for adjustment on the first furlough. Having faced up to the real issues of missionary work in the field, *now* was the time to come to terms with what was seen to be needed. Convictions after this order eventually flowered in the coming into being of the St. Julian's Community.

In the first year of the last war, this sense of God's leading towards the formation of a Community, was very much upon Florence's mind, and upon that of the small group of friends whom she had fired with her idea. They were to work out the life of Christian fellowship together, and provide a place where others could join them in finding a "place of quiet" where they could think things out and find contact with God, renewed in peace and power. Without money and without support they began to search for the right kind of house in the country. Florence resigned from her post with the C.M.S. The other two involved with her equally "burned their boats".

In January 1941, together with a fourth recruit, they started their new career at Oakenrough, Haslemere. The terms of the will under which the previous owner had left the house made it possible for them to use it, as a beginning. The core of the experiment was to work out the two great commandments of Love to God and to one's neighbour as oneself. Starting out on this kind of life, the four speedily discovered "that what we thought we were was a very different picture from what we found ourselves to be". In such close living as was theirs, the problems of human relationship were shown up. Praying—as they discovered—did nothing to ease the situation until there was a willingness to deal with the fault that had arisen in their relationships. It was the lesson of Uganda all over again, and a fresh exposition of the truth behind Matthew 5:23f: "if thou bring thy gift to the altar, and there rememberest that thy brother hath ought against thee, leave then thy gift before the altar, and go thy way, first be reconciled to thy brother, and then come and offer thy gift."

Successive ventures brought them to St. Julian's, Barns Green, which they purchased and furnished almost miraculously. Help and gifts came, and staff to run the experiment. Finally, another house and farm at Coolham were bought at a price of £50,000, and after all manner of discussions and difficulties, they moved in to this property on January 19th, 1950. Of these ten years of running St. Julian's, Florence once commented that this had been "quite the stiffest bit of my life but lovely too". On July 3rd, 1950, after only a few months at Coolham, she died.

Her life illustrates, wonderfully, the quality of Christian faith—the founding of the St. Julian's Community, and the approach to her own illness are supreme examples of this. Her life, too, knew the secret of surrender—of "possession by Christ". "I don't matter to myself any more," was one of the things she said towards the close of her life. She knew the spirit of contemplation: "Keep just looking at God," she said, "not at people. That's the solution—to have a pure capacity for God." "The primary object of prayer is to know God better—we and our needs should be second." She "practised the Presence": "The only way I can learn to do it . . . is to sit quietly before God doing nothing, only fixing the will gently on some expressive word like 'O God, I want Thee', or 'Father', or 'Here am I and here are You'." So much that we have described in other chapters is here in this very lovely life. But the supreme matter illustrated concerns the spirit of reconciliation and forgiveness.

It was the lesson of Uganda, and it was the lesson renewed when the four women started their Christian community at Oakenrough. "I remember a girl writing to me from abroad," said Florence in one of her talks, "telling us how thrilled she was over giving a set of lessons on the Lord's Prayer, and the rest of her letter was spent in blackguarding a certain person with whom she was working. And I thought: 'What will she do—what will she do—when she comes to "forgive us our trespasses as we forgive them that trespass against us"'? I felt frightened," said Florence, "for I knew she would somehow be able to do it."

God keep us from too glibly using that phrase in the Lord's Prayer! In our praying, and in everything else to do with our Christian life, it is of paramount importance that we should learn to deal with resentments and grudges. Love cannot flow into us and through us until those barriers have been removed. God cannot "forgive" us—we cannot be at home in Him— unless we forgive others. Our Lord states the law as categorically as that.

7. AMY CARMICHAEL

DISCOVERING GOD'S WILL FIRST

Lord, what wilt thou have me to do?
ACTS 9: 6

IN 1925 an American woman, Katherine Mayo, began an investigation into Indian life and customs. It resulted in the publication two years later of a book called *Mother India*. Things were revealed in that book that many people had guessed at, and that others had avoided noticing. Amongst the most unpleasant revelations were facts concerning the *devadasses*, temple girls dedicated to the gods. It is in this section of her book that Katherine Mayo mentions both "the extraordinary work" and the "too-reticent books" of Miss Amy Wilson Carmichael.

Amy Carmichael was the last kind of person who would have wished to be faced with the peculiar problems relating both to the temple girls and to the boys of the "drama societies" which she discovered as she worked as a missionary in South India. These "too-reticent books" of hers, though they hint at evils without describing them, yield definite indications of the horror and detestation felt by this refined and saintly woman as she uncovered more and more of the facts regarding these things. Readers of Miss Mayo's books will know that, at least, there is no reticence there.

On March 6th, 1901, in the village of Great Lake, Miss Carmichael, then a Church of England Zenena Society missionary with a background of Keswick religion, met a seven-year-old girl named Pearleyes, who had escaped from a temple in a near-by village. "The child," said Amy, "told us things that darkened the sunlight." Amy's concern for young people caught in this net of bestiality had been awakened.

Wherever she went she gathered more facts about the traffic in children. Two visiting friends from Britain urged her to let them take back with them a manuscript she had already prepared and set aside. This manuscript was the first draft of *Things As They Are*, in which, after an initial chapter or two describing her earlier missionary adventures, she poured out her anguish concerning the temple children. It was the beginning of the enlisting of the concern of other people in this matter.

Sometimes a child is dedicated to the gods because of a vow made by the parents, as for example in the case of a wonderful recovery from illness, or because a widowed mother can no longer support her. "Or," says Katherine Mayo, "a particularly lovely child, for one reason or another held superfluous in her natural surroundings, is presented to the temple." The temple women have their own ways of acquiring recruits. "Everywhere," says Amy Carmichael, "there are men and women on the watch for these children. The sale of a child is illegal; but money is not passed in public, and the necessary proof cannot be obtained."

What could one woman begin to do against this great evil, entrenched in the life of vast areas of Southern India? Much has been done by way of social legislation, and much of this as a direct result of Amy Carmichael's work. But laws do not, and have not, controlled what goes on in secret and under the mask of religion. As Miss Carmichael herself discovered when she began her God-given work in South India, no one would dare the might of the priests and the power of the gods in order to reclaim or shelter even one of the children destined for this traffic. In prayer she had received her commission, and it was in prayer that the whole work that became the "Dohnavur Fellowship" gathered momentum, in spite of all the difficulties and opposition which were encountered.

The Fellowship in South India is now spread over a main site with an area of some 170 acres, comprising buildings and schools for children of both sexes, gardens, fields, a farm and playing fields, a chapel and a hospital for adults, complete with operating theatre, as well as a smaller hospital for the children. In addition there is a house and 37 acres of hillside in the "Forest", as a refuge in the hottest season of the year, and an estate at "Three Pavilions" nearer the sea. "We are a family of nearly seven hundred," Amy Carmichael could write in 1937. And when it all began there was nothing—nothing but a woman's concern and her faith and prayer. Round her a staff and an organisation grew up, round her the Fellowship buildings became established. And it would be true to say that all is a result of prayer, with the centre of it the concern for the saving and reclamation of boys and girls whose lives, had not Dohnavur come into existence, were destined for a life of horror and shame.

In her large book, *Gold Cord*, Amy Carmichael has told of these beginnings and traces the story down to about the year 1931. Other books, as for example the one entitled *Windows*, carry on the story, as she herself saw it.

The first three babies to whom she gave shelter at Dohnavur died. That was discouragement enough. Then, Indian women would not join in the work that meant looking after small children. That was degrading. In spite of manifold difficulties, indeed sometimes because of them, the conviction grew that this work now begun was "in the way of God's leading". And helpers gradually came.

Looking back now, said Amy Carmichael, folk seem to discern a "pattern" in the way that things developed. But there was no pattern for them at the beginning. Need was there, and they answered it, and stage by stage God seemed to show what was the next possibility. Praying about it, they discovered the way opening and the answer coming.

Pappamal was the first to offer for service. She was an Indian girl—the first of her station in Indian society to "demean" herself to work amongst young children. A widow, mourning uselessly, according to the custom, for her dead husband for months on end was the next. She had a dream. "I will send you to a place where they all love one another," said the white-robed visitant who spoke to her in this dream. Within a week a Bishop visiting the near-by church said words to her which, when translated, she recognized as the same words. She scarcely knew how it all happened, but within a few days she and her little boy arrived in Dohnavur. Both mother and son, after the passage of time, proved to be amongst the most useful of helpers in the growing settlement.

Each new step taken in turn in the developing story was under the sense of God's guidance. To begin work amongst boys, after years of rescue work for the girls, was a very bold step indeed. On September 23rd, 1926, Amy notes, "Decision to go on and buy land for boys' compound though no help is in sight", and in the margin of her copy of *Daily Light* she wrote "New land for boys—first advance paid. Help will come. Our God will not forsake us." Later, they discovered, it was on that same day that in China God was liberating Godfrey Webb-Peploe of the C.I.M. Ordered out of that country by the doctors, he was the man destined to take charge of this work amongst boys. On December 15th, he joined them at Dohnavur.

In 1929 they began to build a hospital. For years they had felt certain that their work should enlarge to include medical help for the people of their area. In 1921 they had first felt this clearly. "It was as though there swam into our view a Place of Healing, furnished with all that was required for the help of the people, and we saw the work of the place led by one in whom were the instincts and convictions and the glad abandon of the spiritual pioneer; and the long patience, too." Gifts began to arrive for the building of the new hospital, and on November 15th, 1928, a letter was posted from the R.A. Mess, Meerut, from Dr. Murray Webb-Peploe, Godfrey's elder brother: the man to lead the work was now coming!

On August 15th, 1929, the log-books of Dohnavur record this: "Asked for and received according to 1 John 5: 14f £10,000 for the Place of Healing", and it was signed by all present. In advance they thanked God for what they knew— now they had prayed, by His inspiration, and in Christ's name—would be theirs. It must be remembered that their faith involved that the work amongst the children—their primary commission—should not suffer whilst this extra money was coming in and their extra commitments met. How all this happened is told in *Windows*. The £10,000 came chiefly in small gifts, though Amy tells how on September 2nd, 1929, Murray prayed, privately, for £1,000 "in a single gift". On December 15th a cable "so timed that the spiritual value of that 'single gift' was magnified exceedingly", announced that £1,000 had been given. By December 1935 the amount had been received in full.

For the last twenty years of her life (she died on January 18th, 1951, at the age of 83), Amy was an invalid who rarely left her one room. An accident happened to her in October 1931 from which she never fully recovered. From this room, however, throughout all that time, there poured forth a volume of counsel and leadership, letters, prayers, poems, and books that continued her work and service for God at Dohnavur.

So over the years this family of the Dohnavur Fellowship has grown. Its very existence is a sign and a token. Opposition and difficulty of one sort and another have been encountered, and surmounted. Without presumption, and with tremendous thankfulness, Amy Carmichael could quote—as she does in one of her books—the lines

> I have liv'd
> To see inherited my very wishes,
> And the buildings of my fancy.

"Dream buildings" in themselves are not of much use. It is the faith that knows that the dream is inspired by God that is enabled by prayer and service to see the dream built up on earth. Accounts, as A.C. commented once, are "ruthlessly real". "Dream-money," she says, "pays no bills." She quotes three Tamil proverbs about "dream-provision". They are all in the form of questions which, presumably, all expect the same answer! "Will money seen in a dream pay bills?" "Will wealth seen in a dream reach your hands?" "Will rice eaten in a dream satisfy hunger?" "But", continues this woman of faith, "if the money required to pay the bills comes just as certainly as the bills come, then the fact that it has come is an assurance" that God's blessing is upon what is going forward. He has inspired His people to make provision for what He regards as His work.

The Tamils have another proverb, "No master is responsible for uncommanded work". The joy of the work at Dohnavur, and part of its lesson, in turn, to us, is that it has all been carried through at the bidding of the Unseen Master. All the workers there would agree that His has been the hand that guided, His the heart that planned. "Careless prayer is presumption," says Amy Carmichael, "commanded prayer is obedience." And their praying and venturing forward was all in the line of obedience.

There is a passage at the beginning of *Gold Cord* which brings us to the heart of the matter: "One of the earliest lessons we learned together was that before asking for anything we should find out if it were according to the mind of the Lord. The kind of prayer that is a pouring out of the heart is different. This, that was definite petition, intercession, needed preparation of a special kind. It needed time—time to listen, to understand, to 'wait', as the word is so often in the Psalms. And this is the confidence that we have in Him that *if we ask anything according to His will He heareth us:* and if we know that He hear us whatsoever we ask, *we know that we have* the petitions that we desired of Him."

Here is something of utmost importance. Prayer is of so many kinds—there is, for example, the prayer of communion, when we share our concerns, "pouring out our heart" as Amy Carmichael expresses it. But there is also the prayer of petition that is so certain, so definite, that we can use for it the name suggested by the passage in James 5, and call it the "prayer of faith". It is uttered in that kind of way: it is the kind of prayer that is made believing that we have the things we ask (Matt. 21: 22). It should be noted that, in the passage from James' letter, the illustration he uses is of Elijah, "a man of like passions with ourselves" (he will not appeal to the example of examples, Jesus, but to someone on our own level, an ordinary human being like the rest of us). And from the story in 1 Kings 17 we know this about Elijah's praying that it was prayer *uttered in knowledge.* He knew what God was going to do: and he, as God's agent here upon earth, spoke his faith in prayer. To this kind of praying there is always an answer: but it must be, as Amy Carmichael so clearly describes it, an asking for things "according to the mind of the Lord".

Bishop Frank Houghton in his life of *Amy Carmichael of Dohnavur* quotes a word given by God to Lady Julian of Norwich and set down in the *Revelations of Divine Love.* During the latter period of her life this was a book which became very precious to A.C. Her biographer speaks of this method of prayer based on the assurance that the Spirit will teach us what to pray for, and says that it had become, so to speak, "axiomatic" at Dognavur. For this reason, he says, this word would chime exactly in Amy's mind: "I am the Ground of thy beseeching: first it is my will that thou have it; and after, I make thee to will it; and after, I make thee to beseech it and thou beseechest it. How should it then be that thou shouldest not have thy beseeching?"

There are times when we know that what seems like a good idea to us is not "according to the mind of the Lord". Then, however set we may be on the matter, we do not pray the "prayer of faith" concerning it. We can—and should—discuss it with Him: but we should not, yet, make it a matter of intercession. We cannot do so in the spirit of faith. There is no authority behind our praying.

Quoting, and underlining, the sentence, "We know *that we have* the petitions that we desired of Him", she continues, "We pray from the ground of that certainty: not towards certainty but from it." This, then, we isolate out of the many things that we may learn about prayer from this woman who so greatly proved its efficacy: that before we pray the prayer of definite intercession, in faith, we need first to discover what is the Will of God. A listening, responsive heart and mind, steadied by obedience, is trained in discerning this. Hasty assumptions, or self-induced presumptions, will not do. We must be sure about these petitions in the way that the Lord will make us sure. Then we can go on to pray in a new way altogether. Our praying is then not so much our praying, but the prayer of God in us.

WAYS THAT OPEN

8. MALCOLM SPENCER

The joy of the Lord is your strength.

NEHEMIAH 8: 10

"PERHAPS MALCOLM was as near St. Francis as any we shall ever meet." That is high praise indeed. The same friend who made that statement also likened him to the Pied Piper of Hamelin, to Puck, to Ariel. Malcolm Spencer was, you will gather, a rather unusual figure, worthy of being described, as someone once described Oswald Chambers, as "the most irreverend reverend I ever saw".

His name is not widely known, and, within a few decades, it may pass away altogether, for he was as McEwan Lawson further describes him in the title of a brief biography, "God's Back-room Boy". But those who met him will never forget him: that is equally certain. Long-haired, shabbily dressed, impatient of all such matters, he was a single-eyed visionary concerned with the Kingdom of God. His "back-room" activity concerned itself in endless secretarial work and the organisation of innumerable committees and conferences. The Student Christian Movement and the "Free Church Fellowship" knew him for years in various organizing capacities. Perhaps some of us might think that what could have been an increasingly original contribution was allowed to be lost: snowed under mountains of paper and committee agendas.

75

Malcolm Spencer is introduced into our galaxy of "discoverers in prayer" as an exponent of thanksgiving. He once wrote a pamphlet with the title that stands at the head of this chapter. The book was the outcome of one of the earliest of his conferences. By the sea flats at the tip of Norfolk at a place called Overy Staithe, he gathered with a group of some twenty to thirty friends who belonged to what was then the Primitive Methodist Church. What were they doing? Enjoying a holiday, and at the same time spending their mornings thinking together about prayer. His companions found that Malcolm was opening to them a new world, for he had by this time, as he tells us, "proved the value of taking groups of people over a charted route of thanksgiving". In Malcolm's company, that would be an experience indeed!

The man himself was born in Marple, Cheshire, on 8th May 1877. The family, moving to Manchester, were early plunged into trouble. Malcolm who had lost his mother when three, now lost his father at the age of eight. Eventually, against the background of that family struggle, Malcolm won a scholarship to Manchester Grammar School, and from there another to Corpus Christi, Oxford, where, studying mathematics, he obtained a first. By this time, the S.C.M.—then in its heyday—claimed him. He had determined to become a missionary, but the possibility of going to Africa did not materialise: instead, in 1903 he went to Darwen to be the assistant Congregational minister in that bleak and rather grimy Lancashire town. While there he was allowed to act as "Missionary Campaign Secretary" for the S.C.M., and finally he was invited to become a member of their full-time staff.

Of the days that followed, perhaps this snatch of verse, made to be sung to the tune of "There is a Tavern in the Town" is illustrative. S.C.M. students by the hundred have sung it with gusto at the "Hayes", Swanwick, which houses the annual S.C.M. and many other conferences:

76

> There is a Tavern called the Hayes,
> Where Malcolm Spencer often stays,
> And sits immersed in problems deep,
> And never, never thinks of sleep.

In the year 1931 the S.C.M. published a book from his pen entitled *Vitality*. Perhaps it tells us as much about him as we need to know. Anything, said Malcolm in this book, which has the power to increase life's joy and "speed the spirit of man in his endeavours towards the best and the highest seems to me to be of God". Our concern should be to increase our appreciation, our understanding of, and our participation in, this fund of vitality which comes from Him.

In order to quicken this spirit in us, we should "go the whole round of creation" from its lowest to its highest form of life and cultivate the power to rejoice in all of them. . . . Beginning anywhere and stopping nowhere, we praise God for all that is beautiful in life. It is when we come to his suggested "daily regimen" that we realise how different this modern St. Francis is from the rest of us. It begins: "On getting up put your head out of your window and take a real look at the sky, not just to see if rain is likely, but to realise its infinitude and its capacity for beauty. Then whether or no you can take a cold bath with your present degree of vitality, strip naked and so remain for some time; and in that time do something to stretch the body and feel the joy of physical life. . . . Then when you are physically alert and gay, after a good towelling, the mind can be attuned to come into its own. . . ." The suggestions end thus: "And if, at any hour of the day, you catch your spirit slumbering and some side of your nature asleep or aloof from the fascination of life, awaken it with a douse of cold water, or the shaking of limbs, an ejaculation of praise, a renewal of vows, or a snatch of song, or dance . . . do anything, or everything that will reinstate you as a person wholly alive in an exacting but very delectable world."

One can understand how surprised some of his hosts and hostesses must have been when Malcolm came to stay with them as a special preacher or deputation to some conference or other. Before the rest of the world was awake, he was to be seen out on the lawn doing somersaults, or leaping over bushes for sheer joy, running down to the near-by pond or river, and plunging in; then he would spend some time, kneeling, or sometimes lying prostrate on the ground, remembering his friends and all the causes he had so much on his heart in prayer.

Malcolm himself loved to tell of the summer morning at five o'clock when, now past forty and living at Harrow, clad in vest and lilac-coloured shorts, he was returning from his early morning run, and found that he was without his latch-key. Rather than disturb the family, he decided to borrow the long garden ladder from next door and enter through an upstairs window. Just when he was carrying out this operation, a burly policeman came into view. The latter halted in his tracks, perceptibly shaken by the vision that met him. Malcolm found it very difficult to persuade the policeman that he was the rightful owner of the house into which he seemed to be breaking. "Officer," he suggested, finally, "if you will climb this ladder you will find it leads to the bathroom. In the bathroom, just above the basin, you will find a glass containing a set of dentures. If you will bring these you will find that they fit me." The policeman would not forget that morning encounter any more than would others who met this unusual man at unusual times doing unusual things.

What Malcolm Spencer had discovered is that this world is a vast wonderland, in which, unfortunately, most people are half-awake, living unnecessarily impoverished lives. Always a campaigner for social righteousness and, especially since his Darwen days, desperately keen for a fair share of life and beauty for everyone, he yet saw that the supreme need for each man was that he should be awakened from within to what already lay around him. Finding strength and inspiration from fellow-ship with other Christians and from partaking in common worship, it yet seemed to him that many churches were half-dead, with no lift about them and no consciousness of living in the days of the Resurrection. For Malcolm they were too gloomy, both in their outlook and in their furnishings and architecture. More light, more colour, more beauty is what he longed for.

To return to *Thanksgiving—The Key to Prayer*: this was originally to have been a book on Intercession; but, like Dr. Johnson's Mr. Edwards, who would have been a philosopher had not cheerfulness kept breaking in, the book did not get as far as that, and turned out to be a book on Thanksgiving! This fact in itself is indicative of a truth that Malcolm had proved over and over again: for one is quite sure that in those sessions in the morning, whether on the lawn, or by the sea, or in his room when, after his exercises, Malcolm remembered his friends before God, thanksgiving rich and deep would be his first thought in prayer. This man came to discover more and more that this spirit holds the key to all the rest of prayer. It sets us in the proper frame for everything that follows. It tunes us in to God.

"It seems to me both impertinent and exhausting," he wrote, "to attempt to mobilise the spiritual forces of the universe for the betterment of the world, till we are overflowing with appreciation of the works of God in the world as it is. The contemplation of God's goodness is the proper source of energy for all our asking, and the proper guide to us in choosing what we shall ask."

It is noteworthy that St. Paul in his Letters often counselled the folk of his day similarly. "Continue steadfastly in prayer," he writes, "watching therein with thanksgiving"; "Giving thanks always for all things". He brings his first Letter to the Thessalonians to a close in this way: "Rejoice alway, pray without ceasing, in everything give thanks: for this is the will of God in Christ Jesus to you." "Maintain your zest for prayer," says the apostle (in Moffatt's translation of Colossians 4:2), "with thanksgiving."

Halyburton, than whom it is scarcely possible to imagine a greater contrast to Malcolm Spencer—sombre Scottish puritan as over against someone emancipated from all that is sombre in puritanism—tells us in his *Memoirs* that he, too, made a great discovery. "I have found a law," he says, "that always, even when at the lowest deeps, I can pull myself back into the sunshine through the duty of thankfulness."

There is no way like Thanksgiving to put us in tune. It makes us think of God, instead of ourselves: of His power, and love, instead of our weakness and failure. It is one of the greatest cures for spiritual malaise. It is, as Malcolm Spencer describes it, "the key to prayer".

9. STUDDERT KENNEDY AND REBECCA BEARD

PRAYING IN PICTURES

What things soever ye desire, when ye pray, believe that ye receive them, and ye shall have them.

MARK 11: 24

HOW DO you pray? Using words—silently, or perhaps out loud? Or do you pray mentally, using abstract ideas? Or perhaps you pray in pictures? People vary much in these matters. It is quite certain, however, that many people can be tremendously helped by the suggestion that they might try the method of "praying in pictures".

It is a method which can be used in two main ways: (1) to bring us consciously into the presence of God and to link us with some great gospel truth or incident, and (2) to help to make clear, in our imagination, just what it is that we are seeking when we pray. We can forepicture the answer.

Studdert Kennedy, "Woodbine Willie" of the First World War, discovered the usefulness of this method more particularly from the first point of view. Towards the end of his all-too-brief career, in his I.C.F. missions, he would encourage the people present to join him in an act of this kind. Let Ronald Sinclair, who has described this method under the title *When we Pray*, paint the picture of the close of one of these services. For forty minutes, the congregation have been listening spell-bound to the words of this dynamic Irishman, clad in well-worn black cassock. "Woodbine Willie" has been speaking of the

Cross, in which both the Love of God and the sin of man are exposed, made clear, for all time. Suddenly he breaks off. Leaving the place from which he has been speaking, and walking swiftly into the aisle, he kneels amongst the people. "Let us go into the silent place," he says. It is a signal understood by the congregation, for they have been following it since the first night of the mission.

After a space of silence, the soft Irish voice continues: "We will take as our picture Jesus on the Cross, broken, yet triumphant, so weak, yet so strong, so marred, yet so beautiful, so human and yet so divine." Studdert Kennedy draws a picture of the Crucified which makes a deep impression on the imagination of all present. After a space, in which all are invited to worship and adore, the voice breaks in again: "Now go out"—and he means the kind of going out that is in thought and imagination—"and fetch into the Silent Place those who are groping in the darkness of the world, broken men and women. . . ." It is a form of praying for others that has special power about it. The congregation sees those broken people come, for it has summoned them . . . and it sees them go again, after being in His Presence, the Crucified. They are changed men and women. They have pictured it all, vividly, for themselves.

Ronald Sinclair developed Studdert Kennedy's method into something of a system, showing its efficacy as a way for private prayer, too. We are to begin by remembering our Lord's advice: "when thou prayest, enter into thine inner chamber, and having shut thy door, pray to thy Father which seeth in secret". We start, then, by preparing an inner sanctuary, a secret place. This we deliberately set out to do, making a picture of what, for us, shall in future be that "secret place". Henceforth it exists in our imagination, and can be conjured up immediately. It may be a room, or perhaps an outside scene, perhaps an impression of Galilee, or the hills beyond Nazareth, or perhaps a spot in our own beloved Lakeland. It is a place which we share with Jesus. It is our "secret place" of prayer.

An essential element in this kind of praying is to wait, always to wait, for Him. He is the Living Christ, who will come to our trysting-place. We shall know when He has entered and thereafter our prayer is a co-operative venture.

In the "sanctuary", and in the communion begun, we can continue by choosing a further picture. It may be a scene from the Gospels—Jesus stilling the storm, or blessing the little children, or washing the disciples' feet. The picture will call out our adoration; and it can provide a framework, too, into which we can fit our intercessions and our concerns for others.

We have said that many people find this suggestion of great value: it is especially true of people not trained or fitted for abstract thinking and reasoning, and folk not gifted at expressing themselves in words. "Thinking in pictures" is something which reaches the deepest strata in our mental make-up. Millennia before man learnt to reason, or to express his thoughts in words, in memory he could recall what he had seen, and he could set his imagination to work, particularly at times of great hope or peril, to conjure up pictures of possibilities in the future. McNeile Dixon makes the point graphically when he reminds us that "the human mind is not, as philosophers would have us think, a debating hall, but a picture gallery".

This has much to say to us about the kind of praying that has an answer. Strongly held pictures deep in the mind are themselves a kind of prayer—whatever our words may be, this is the real picture we are holding of the future: this is what we believe will happen: this is where our faith really lies.

Rebecca Beard was an American doctor who after twenty years of *materia medica* turned to a more spiritual and psychosomatic dealing with illness. She has described how she found that the mental pictures that folk carry in the mind are of utmost importance as factors working either towards health or disease.

She discovered this as a working principle, both in her own experience, and in that of her patients. She discusses this in her books, and notably in the one entitled *Everyman's Adventure*.[1]

First, however, let me recount something of Dr. Rebecca Beard's story. She tells us that, in her early years, she knew little of organised religion. Her father was a free-thinker. Her mother, descended from a long line of Wesleyan ministers, sent her children to Sunday School and read the Bible to them. But, when she went to college to study chemistry and physics, it was Science that became her religion. The idea of the dependability and rationality of the natural order was impressed on her mind. The "laws of nature" were unchangeable and all-controlling.

The steps by which Rebecca passed "from *materia medica* to spiritual therapy" are enthralling. They are outlined at the beginning of her first book, *Everyman's Search*. Work in the dispensary of the hospital first revealed to her that there was a magic at work in connection with the drugs that she dispensed. The "drug of the moment", acclaimed on all sides, would seem to possess, for a time, a special potency, and then it would pass out of use. The effect of the coming of "the Doctor" to a patient's bedside also held a magic—especially that of some doctors, and in the case of some patients. Then, the visit of a loved one, a friend, or a pastor to the bedside of a patient desperately ill often held some magic, too. Once in a while a patient not expected to live would get better. There were these unknown factors at work, factors which had to do with intangible things like faith, and prayer, imagination, hope, love, sorrow. For Rebecca, as for so many medical people in recent years, the revelations of psychology and psychosomatic medicine brought in a new dimension. Medicine was being liberated from the chains of the merely material.

[1] Published by Arthur James (Evesham).

What finally brought. Rebecca "from *materia medica* to spiritual therapy" was, however, the ultimatum bluntly given to the Doctor herself one day: "You must put your affairs in order, Doctor. You cannot live through another heart attack."

"Faith", says Florence Allshorn in words we have already quoted, "is not an easy thing to come by. You are fortunate if you have been ill enough to think that only faith will save you. Then you have to have it." Florence knew that for herself, and now so did Rebecca Beard. It was only then, she says, "that God became real, and I began to sense the great power that was outside of myself, and yet was part of me, and I cried, 'If it is possible, take this from me. Either take it from me or take me. I have gone as far as I can'". Then it was that she knew a "great spiritual illumination" and at the same time knew that she was healed. The rest of her life would be given in helping others to find healing after this manner.

The way of that future service was settled in meetings with Glenn Clark and others in conferences concerning what together they called "Healing Advance". In the spring of 1947 Rebecca and her husband gave up their home and went to a place called Merrybrook. It was to be a home where they could receive patients seeking "spiritual therapy". In the years since there have been a number of cures at Merrybrook of (medically speaking) apparently hopeless cases, and they have learned a great deal concerning prayer and meditation, and the influence of spiritual factors on the lives of their patients. Rebecca herself, told as she had been by her medical colleagues back in 1945 that she would never survive another heart attack, lived for many years as a shining example of what "spiritual therapy" can do.

Her own philosophy was built squarely upon her scientific and medical training. "You don't change the laws of chemistry and physics when you come into the realm of biology and psychology," she wrote. "The difference is that in biology and psychology you introduce the factors of human life and that changes the relationship of all the other factors involved." So it is when still higher laws and powers come into operation. The "lower" laws are not abrogated. They come into relationship with these still higher factors. Prayer belongs to the realm of the higher laws and is not magic: it is "the orderly operation of a vital energy". By means of it we are in touch with the creative Life of God. Willingness to receive is part of the preparation for this vital prayer. Removal of the barriers which prevent our openness to Him is also necessary. Many are the truths concerning prayer which this medical woman came to discover in her own experience and in dealing with others.

Lack of forgiveness, the harbourings of grudges and resentments, inevitably meant a barrier to healing, for the reasons that we have already observed in earlier chapters. Holding to the wrong picture of the future Rebecca Beard found to be another barrier. In this case, imagination is being used *against* cure rather than for it. Common phrases reveal the existence of such negative pictures in our deeper mind: "Of course, I don't expect to get better." "I shall never be any good." "If I had the health and vitality that so-and-so has." . . .

Rebecca Beard noted what psychology has to say about the influence of paramount ideas in the subconscious mind, and of what Coué and others have revealed concerning the relative strength of the imagination and the will: "Should the imagination and the will be in conflict, it is always the imagination that wins." To anyone concerned with spiritual therapy, all this is of the utmost significance. As Rebecca came to know in dealing with one patient after another, it was no use the patient, for example, affirming, "I will stand up straight. I will not have any pain in my side," if at the same time the imagination was still dwelling on that very twinge, and on the inability to stand up straight. The image of the pain, in this set of circumstances, is far stronger than any set of ideas to do with cure.

It is only if your picture, made in faith and imagination, is *stronger* than the prior picture of pain and imperfection that the subconscious mind, which affects the health of the body, will take any notice. You can "affirm" what you like, but it is the stronger picture—the real picture you are forming—whether positive or negative, that counts.

Prayer enables the positive picture to become stronger, and finally to become dominant, since it is rooted in God and in His good will for us—this is what Rebecca Beard discovered and taught. Said she, we need to invite God to cleanse our subconscious mind, to render those negative impressions impotent, and to make this deeper part of our nature receptive to the "infilling of healthy, positive imagery". Then it is that we can fill our waking minds—our normal consciousness—with pictures that are not at variance with what our imagination is saying deep down in our "subconscious". Throughout these realms, absolute honesty must hold. It is no use "affirming" one thing, and "believing" another. Our hopes and aspirations must be at one, through and through. This is the point at which prayer, and God's dealing with us as a result of it, becomes so vital.

What we have to do then, says Rebecca Beard, is "to visualize, to make a picture of what we want". This, as we have noticed, is not so much the first use we suggested of "praying in pictures". Studdert Kennedy and Ronald Sinclair make of this a means of preparation for communion with God, and a way of meditation. What we are now considering is the fore-picturing of what it is we desire of life and of God, for ourselves and for others. (There is no reason, of course, why the two methods should not be combined, as indeed they often have been.)

"What wilt thou that I should do unto thee?" said Jesus to

blind Bartimaeus. On the face of it, it seems a foolish question —does not the man's struggle to get to Jesus, blind as he was, make it obvious what he wanted? But in that moment when Jesus asks His question, blind Bartimaeus *sees* what it is to see. He knows, with all his heart, as never before, just what it is he wants. Uttermost desiring brought to an absolute focus is behind this forepicturing as he cries, "Lord that I may receive my sight." "Receive thy sight," says the Lord: "thy faith hath made thee whole." And immediately, he received his sight, and followed Him, glorifying God.

10. PAUL CLAUDEL

THE DEPTHS IN OUR NATURE

Deep calleth unto deep.
PSALM 42: 7

IN 1942 Gallimard, the Parisian publishers, put out a book
entitled *Seigneur Apprenez-Nous à Prier*. It was by Paul
Claudel. During the closing years of his life this most unusual
man, diplomat, poet, playwright, confined his writing almost
entirely to religious themes. Of all these books this short work
is not the least remarkable. Ruth Bethell translated it into
English, and in 1947 it was published[1] in London. The book
is illustrated by some reproductions of French and Flemish
paintings. These together with the illuminative comments and
evocative ideas set out in the text provide a book on prayer
different from any other that the present writer has encountered.
They seem especially to emphasize the possibility of communing
with God in the depths of our nature. God can come to us
there, cleansing those depths within us, and there making
Himself known and working through us.

Paul Claudel was born in 1868 at Villeneuve-sur-Fère, in
the heart of agricultural France, in the Tardinois. Fourteen
years later his family moved to Paris, where Paul attended the
lycée Louis-le-Grand. The boy surrendered quickly to the
prevalent materialistic, mechanistic view of life, and lost the
ardent, first-hand sense of joy that he had known in the more
simple life of the countryside.

[1] By Dennis Dobson Ltd.

89

On Christmas Day, 1886, this youth, now undergoing a swift artistic development, and secretly yearning for something other than the "materialist prison" in which he felt himself to be held, paid what was meant to be a casual visit to the great Cathedral of Notre-Dame. Vespers were in progress. What happened was that, then and there, in the Cathedral, he was converted. It was in the singing of the Magnificat that it happened. In his poem "The Magnificat" he describes it in this way:

And lo! You were Somebody all of a sudden.

"In one instant," he declared in another place, "my heart was touched and I believed. I believed with such a strength of adherence, with such a profound conviction, with such a certitude, that there was no room for any sort of doubt."

His goal as a student was the diplomatic service, and to prepare for that he attended the Ecole du Droit and the Ecole des Sciences Politiques. As a writer of great promise, he was welcomed into Parisian literary circles, and wrote three outstanding plays before he started on his career as a diplomat. In 1893 he travelled to America, becoming Vice-Consul in Boston. In 1896 he was appointed Consul in Foochow, where the strange, secret life of China exercised a deep influence upon him.

A most interesting episode in Claudel's life occurred in the year 1900. He was, as we have suggested, someone who in turn was man of affairs, poet, and man of religion. When he returned first from the East, at the turn of the century, he put his call as "man of religion" to the test. Since he was a Roman Catholic, this meant entering a monastery or offering for the priesthood. In September 1900, he entered the Abbey of Ligugé as a novice in the Benedictine order. As he continued praying earnestly about this matter, he received a definite assurance that this life was not God's plan for him. Conversation with his superiors in the monastery confirmed this to him. He believed that he had his answer and thereafter never questioned it. He was now free to continue his artistic vocation and his diplomatic activities. So, in 1901, he returned to China.

In 1909, now married, he returned to Europe, serving in the Consulates at Prague, Frankfurt and Hamburg. He was French Ambassador in Tokyo from 1921 to 1927. Then, as Ambassador in Washington from 1927, he negotiated the Kellog-Briand pact; finally ending his diplomatic career in Brussels as Ambassador in 1936.

During all this time he continued his writing. Some have ventured to call Claudel "the greatest religious poet since Dante". Such plays as *The Tidings Brought to Mary, The Hostage* and *The Satin Slipper* are certainly among the great plays of this generation, though, because of difficulties of production, they have rarely been performed—in fact, they never were performed at all until the days of the German occupation!

Two volumes of Claudel's letters have been translated into English. The first was *Letters to a Doubter*, which covers the correspondence between him and Jacques Rivière. The latter was a critic and literateur who asked Claudel to help him in his search for God: "I long to feel Him present, here, close to me, solid and unmistakable. . . . Give me your answer, and with it peace." The letters concern the clearing away of intellectual difficulties, the probing of secret insincerities, and the gradual winning of a soul from negation and meaninglessness to affirmation and assurance. Rivière is afraid to commit himself too easily lest such a course should prove to be a cowardly evasion of life's struggle and debate. Claudel replies, "Dear friend, the day you receive God you will have a Guest within you who will never leave you repose. He brings a sword. On that day you will know a ferment no earthly vessel can contain." The correspondence ends with Rivière brought into the fold. "On

Christmas Day," he reports quietly to Claudel, "I took communion in Notre Dame."

Claudel's attempts to win André Gide for Catholicism did not have so definite a result, though there is no question that he influenced the other writer far more than he was willing to acknowledge. There came a time, actually, when the battle was almost won. The second volume of letters, then, is that of *The Correspondence 1899–1926* between these two, translated by John Russell.[1]

Gide's *Journal* for 1st December 1905 gives us a portrait of Claudel: "As a young man he looked like a nail: now he looks like a sledge-hammer. Not a very high forehead, but rather wide; face without subtilty as if chiselled out; bull neck continued by the straight line of the head, through which passion can rush to the brain. Yes, I think this is the dominating impression: the head is of one piece with the body .... He gives me the impression of a solidified cyclone. When he talks, it is as if something were released within him; he proceeds by sudden affirmations and maintains a hostile tone even when you share his opinion." That description tells us a very great deal about the man.

These letters emphasise some of the points already made: the first, that the Christian life is not one of absence of struggle. In a letter to Gide from Tientsin, dated 8th July 1909, Claudel writes, "The Christian does not live in a state of equilibrium like the sages of old, but in a state of conflict. Every one of his acts has its consequences; he feels himself in a continual state of re-adaptation. No goad is as sharp as the truth; the life of St. Paul after his conversion was not the life of a man who complacently takes his ease. Even Christ was tempted. And from the intellectual point of view, what a heroic stimulus for the mind is there for us in all those revelations which we have got to understand."

[1] Published by Secker and Warburg 1952.

Then there is Claudel's insistence that what happens in conversion is that the life of God comes to birth within us. Something is going forward to which we give our approval, and to which we willingly make ourselves the host. In a letter from Tokyo, dated 12th January 1924, he states, "The Kingdom of God . . . begins growing and working: somebody is being nourished within us, and within us, at our expense, he carries out his mysterious task of transformation. Of this task, our souls and our bodies are the elements; and the task ends when we are resurrected entire. The Christian is the man who gives himself over completely to the surreptitious construction of a new life, who asks for nothing but this imposition, who no longer has a life of his own; but it is Christ who lives in him. Sainthood consists in cutting down the partition, in abolishing oneself, in ceasing to offer any obstacle to the will of God."

In 1925, coming home from the Far East, Claudel met with two Carmelite nuns on board ship. He confesses that his conversations with them, and his knowledge of their intercession for him, helped him forward in grasping the full possibilities of prayer. He had always thought of it as a way of abandoning oneself completely, profoundly, and as a son, to the Will which is within us. For him, as for Stanley Jones and Kagawa, the initial secret of prayer was surrender. Now, however, it seems that he was awakened to the enormous power of prayer in an altogether new fashion, and especially of this form of praying in which we "get ourselves out of the way" (to use Glenn Clark's phrase) and cease to offer, by our own wilfulness and self-centred desiring, any obstacle to the will of God.

Claudel writes from Chuzenji on 25th July 1926 to tell Gide of this. Older folk, he says, with deep meaning, can understand much better than younger people the point of the parable of the pearl of great price! For them, the treasures of the years, all of them greatly valued, are let go when one is in sight of the one great jewel! "I know now," he says, "what I grasp tightly in my hand when I am quite alone, I dare to relax my grip a little. After forty years, and thanks to the intervention of the two holy Carmelites of Cholet, the gates of prayer have opened for me. I am like one of those little ragged men who used to be sent out on the roads of France to sweep away horse droppings. One summer day the great gate with its lofty barriers of sheet-iron before which he carried out his duties, was no longer shut, but open. At first he only looked inside; then he took a few steps forward on the miraculous gravel, only to run hastily back; then he takes a chance and goes as far as the geranium bed, and in the great silence of the afternoon he hears the sounds of water being sprayed on the heavenly lawns, and in the distance a river running with a muffled roar. Tomorrow, and the next day, will the gate be open? It will! And in the end he understands that the gates have been opened for him.

"They are open for you, too," Claudel continues. "Don't bother about the lodge-keeper. Just don't look at him, and he won't see you."

Long after this Claudel wrote the little book on prayer to which we have referred, *Lord, Teach us to Pray*. Its value lies in the fact that it is written by someone for whom "the gates of prayer had opened".

He begins by referring to Jules Verne's novel, *The Mysterious Island*. The people shipwrecked on the island receive help at crucial moments. A fire is lit for them, a box of tools is discovered on the beach, from the top of an unscalable rock a rope descends to them. Cyrus Smith, an engineer, is not willing, like others in the party, to accept this apparent collaboration without investigation. The first picture in the book is an engraving of "L'Explorateur"—Cyrus is hanging on to a rope ladder let down into a dark well into whose depths, lit by the lantern he holds in his hand, he peers, thinking that he has detected some slight movement. It is, indeed, by this channel that Captain Nemo emerges from his deep-sea retreat in order to observe human beings once again and to listen to their voices.

Says Claudel, we are in a situation curiously parallel—helped in all manner of ways at crucial moments, with our wants and needs anticipated and supplied. The way of discovery by which we come into living touch with our Unseen Helper is not unconnected, either, with what is suggested in the picture of "L'Explorateur".

The second picture is that of "The Key", by Nicolas Maes. Against a dark background an old woman sits at the base of a pillar, reading. Behind her is a niche in which is a bust, representing "Grief", with a flask beside it ("containing distilled wisdom"). On the table are more books. But the central item in the picture is a large key. The full light of the picture, and the weight of its composition, falls on it as it hangs on the wall. As Claudel lets this picture speak to us perhaps the idea that most impresses is that, in a way, we know that that key is irrelevant. It hangs there not because it is necessary, but just because it is no longer needed at all. Whatever door it opens is already accessible to "the specialist in closed doors. ADAM, WHERE ART THOU?" I am reached, deep within my nature by one who—with the key or without it—has access to my deeper nature.

Rembrandt's "Philosopher" is the third in this group of reproductions. You know the picture? The philosopher is seated in a place where many ways intersect. It is not a shut room that he is in. He sits back from his book at the moment we look at him, deep in meditation. The sun streams in through the window in front. Beyond him, a cloistered passage-way extends, and again to the left there is another passage. But the most striking feature in the whole picture is the curving stairway going out of the picture on the far left. Two branches of the stairway are indicated, one going up from the level on which we are, and the other coming down from the flight above. Light—Rembrandtian light—shines on to the first steps leading upwards, and on to the curve of the descending stairs. It is out in the gloom beyond the picture that the branches of the stairway meet. "Thus it is," comments Claudel, "that Jacob's ladder has been compressed to a size to suit the old fellow's convenience."

The effect of these pictures, taken one after the other, is to add strength to Claudel's quotation of the phrase, "THE KINGDOM OF GOD IS WITHIN US"[1] "To think," he says, "that all the time we have within us this inexhaustible source of strength and knowledge, this resource of immortality, and make no effort to discover it."

We make our supreme mistake in voyaging throughout the world in our search for truth and meaning, for light and power, digging in remote and inaccessible places, while all the time the rich vein, the golden ore is here in the depth of our nature. It is also true, thanks be to God, that, where all the intersections of life converge, there God comes down to greet us. Jacob's ladder is let down to us where we are. And when we allow ourselves to be quiet in meditation, deep within our nature, we can have fellowship and communion with God.

Somebody, says Claudel, has found us there. "Why not save him half his journey and meet him half way?" Changing the metaphor: it is true that within ourselves we have access

---

[1] We need not enter here into the discussion about the text which Claudel quotes so decisively. As a French Catholic he quotes, of course, from the Douai version, where the words of Luke 17: 21 are translated in this way. The original Greek phrase, which we can anglicize as *entos humōn*, can be translated either as "amongst you" or "within you", for the preposition *entos* can carry either meaning. But in whatever sense the words were originally used, there cannot be any doubt that they are full of meaning in the form that Claudel, and so many others, have understood them. The pagan philosopher, Marcus Aurelius, knew that the source of inspiration is the same direction: "Look within," he counselled. "Within is the fountain of good, and it will ever bubble up if thou wilt ever dig." It is here that God is known. This is the place of vital contact, in prayer.

to an inexhaustible spring. We need not try to eke out our creative life as from an ebbing cistern. As our Lord says, we can "drink of Him", and find that He in us becomes a "fountain of living waters" The place to make this contact, and to find the waters of renewal, is within ourselves.

There are two aspects to this communion, this type of praying by which we find contact with God deep within our own nature. "The soul needs to pray in the same way as we need to eat and breathe and sleep," says Claudel. With the greatest "naturalness" in the world, then, we can slip into the life of God in prayer, and in that infinite silence lose our littlenesses, our pettiness, our sin, and find His ocean of forgiveness, peace and power swirling our smallness away and reviving in us His true life. This is the one side of prayer.

But, as in all else in life, there is the alternating rhythm. There is rest and relaxation, on the one side, and tension and effort on the other. Rejuvenated as we are in prayer in God's presence we find energy coming into us which must express itself in the other aspect of prayer. This makes of prayer itself sometimes a matter of striving, even of battle. As well as submitting to Him, we are called upon to co-operate creatively with Him. The very life He breathes into us has its own glorious quality of independence. We make our requests, then—and make them in the greatest detail. "Ask," He says, "and you shall receive." "That is what He came for, to ask us to ask and not to cease asking nor to cease being towards Him all desire and aspiration." "God within the framework of His general intention, is for ever acting through individual wills."

> Grant that at last I may be
> All that which within me is obscurely desired.

The way forward is in the coming to birth of creative desire for ourselves and for others. Claudel's invitations to prayer after this order are in the heroic mould: "Drink long and deep of this proof of your own existence," he says. "Don't be afraid if, in the depths of your soul, a plug gives way and a spring rushes in to join the brook."

When Claudel, as a Catholic, out of his own long experience and reflection, talks like this, we find that he is in tune with the most Protestant among us. He has found the place of vital communion. It is not in external things, not in ritual acts done in the world outside us, but here in the depths of our own nature where, by faith, we find personal and living touch with Him, and whence, in the rhythm of asking and receiving, the life of prayer goes forward.

11. LILIAN BAYLIS

The Prayer of Demand

Men ought always to pray, and not to faint (not give up).
LUKE 18: 1

BROTHER LAWRENCE, in one of his *Conversations*, speaks of his "Practice of the Presence of God" as "begetting a holy freedom with God". God's children are as diverse as the human race, and some of them have a large streak of independence and daring in them. It is good, sometimes, to note how bold, and how simple in their boldness, some of God's saints can be. The "energy" in prayer, the creative independence, the deep desiring which Paul Claudel analyses as part of prayer comes strongly to life in these people. And the God who bids us ask, honours these bold seekers in their asking.

It is Dame Sybil Thorndike, who spent some years with Lilian Baylis at the Old Vic, who suggests to us that we might think of counting that extraordinary personality as among the "saints". Few of us might have thought of her in that category had not Dame Sybil first made the suggestion. She obviously came to think of Miss Baylis in this way through playing the part of St. Joan, and understanding what it was that George Bernard Shaw was saying through his portrayal of that most unconventional character. "She was miraculous—and she was unbearable," Shaw comments concerning her. Sybil Thorndike makes it clear that the comment would equally

99

have covered the manager and lessee of the Old Vic! She recounts that one day Lilian Baylis said to her about St. Joan, "Fancy a girl like that being able to face generals, kings and bishops and make them do what she knew was right," and then she went on, very significantly—"it's difficult enough with the Vic, but thinking of Joan is a help to me."

Sybil Thorndike quotes the passage from Shaw's play about Joan's voices. "Oh! your voices, your voices," the Dauphin says irritably to her. Just as surely, though in other words, people retorted to Lilian about the certainties which she knew had come to her. Once she had received an intuition like this "at the altar" she held to it, come what may.

> "I hear voices telling me what to do—they come from God."
> "They come from your imagination," said Robert de Baudri-court.
> "Of course," answered Joan, "that's how the messages of God come to us."

"I never said those words," comments Sybil Thorndike, "without thinking of Lilian."

Lilian Baylis took over the "Old Vic" from her aunt, Miss Emma Cons, who had rescued the place in 1879. This theatre, originally opened in 1818, was re-named in Queen Victoria's girlhood "The Royal Victoria Theatre", which was shortened to "The Vic" and inevitably, in that Waterloo Road and New Cut district, soon affectionately referred to as the "Old Vic".

In Queen Victoria's golden days, The Vic was a music-hall so disreputable that the police gave it a wide berth! Under Emma Cons not only was the building reconstructed, but everything about it was completely changed. It became a "Temperance Music Hall", where lectures and "penny readings" were given. Twenty years later, Lilian Baylis began her management there, and introduced productions of Opera in English. "She was always adventuring," said Sybil

Thorndike of her. "She had no 'settling down' in her composition." This was the first of her major adventures. After her aunt's death in 1912, under the Governors, Lilian took entire charge, and in 1914, against all advice and in spite of mounting difficulties, started performances of Shakespeare's plays at the Old Vic.

What were her motives in all this? Lilian Baylis had, first of all, an enormous love for the people in the midst of whom the Old Vic was set. Without any question, in those early days she felt a concern, through the medium of her theatre, to introduce to as many of them as would have it not only some of the treasures of the operatic world but also those great plays which Lilian herself knew could do something for the human spirit. At a price low enough to make it possible for everybody, she wanted Londoners to enjoy straightforward performances of the classics.

I remember, in my younger days, going down to the New Cut, and entering that dimly lit, ramshackle old theatre to see a play, or to listen to "Figaro" or "Aida". Never shall I forget some of those experiences—the first taste given to me, as a young Londoner, of some of the great things of music and imagination. One could get in, in those days, for a few coppers. Nor shall I forget some of the ill-fitting singers one saw there, nor the expedients which the production were obviously put to with their meagre resources—e.g. the Grand March in Aida, with the same eight or ten men, marching in and out of the stage in ever-new formations, trying to look different! Nor do I forget, over the years, one's cheerful cockney neighbours, and especially the crowd in the gallery, and the smell of oranges, and the inscription on all the notices, "Lessee: Lilian Baylis". How much those folk thought of her! She was the great panjandrum behind all this magic, and, as I heard her once described, "no end of a one" into the bargain. About the Old Vic, her will was law. And if she was prepared to strike out on some new line, then nothing in heaven or earth would stop her.

After her death—which occurred dramatically in November 1937, just before an already-postponed production of *Macbeth*, with Laurence Olivier in the leading rôle—Dame Sybil Thorndike and her brother, Russell, wrote a tribute to her, in which both spoke, in turn, of "Lilian Baylis as I knew her". Their view of her is understanding and kindly. Not everyone saw her in that way. St. John Ervine, in an article which appeared a few days after her death, denigrated her as someone ill-educated, stingy, domineering, prudish and rude, with no business sense at all! Norman Marshall, in a chapter in his book, *The Other Theatre*, says that she was "one of the strangest figures in the whole history of the English theatre. 'Strange'," he continues, "may seem a curious word to apply to that homely, dumpy, spectacled figure with her cockney accent, her deep sense of religion and her rough, humorous tongue: nevertheless it is very strange that a woman in every way so ill-equipped for her task should have succeeded in doing so much."

It is perhaps strangest of all to find this particular woman in the setting of a theatre! She seems to be a misfit. Sybil Thorndike has the clue when she says that the audience at the Old Vic were a "real congregation to Lilian". It is odd to notice the kind of phrases that people use about her and her work. J. C. Trewin, writing of *The Theatre since 1900*, says that in the 1920's Lilian Baylis "a strange, inspiring personality of the theatre who has left no carbon-copy, was turning her coffee-and-culture house from a kind of South London Mission into one of the most honoured theatres in London".

Russell Thorndike tells us of his first interview with this legendary character, the picture of whose oddity had been built up from what his sister had told him of her and her methods of running a theatre. Russell had been invalided home from the Dardanelles in 1916. He received many kindnesses from the lessee of the Old Vic. At certain times a car was put at his disposal, by means of which he could be taken for afternoon drives. One of these drives took him, willy-nilly, to the Old Vic, where he was lifted up the stairs and laid on the sofa in Miss Baylis's room.

It seemed that, at the time, she was concerned about putting on a production of "Henry V". Before Russell knew what was happening, he discovered that she was inviting him to join her in prayer. "I believe in prayer, Dear Boy," she said. "I'm sure God must be sick of me and my worries, because I never decide on anything here, till I've asked God what is best. I get everybody to pray with me for the Vic, but I've never yet prayed with a soldier just home from the front, and I'm sure God will listen to a soldier. That's why I wanted you to be here today. We must pray together to find us soldierly men for this play."

Perhaps we are nearer now to understanding something of the secret of this woman's success in a field to which some judged her to be so ill-suited! Something other than a "business-sense" is at work here!

Russell Thorndike's description of her prayer is inimitable: "She then knelt down by the roll-top desk, with one hand resting upon the base of the telephone. The prayer which followed was exactly like a business talk over the phone. The 'Dear God' she addressed seemed to be at the other end of the line. She told Him who she was and what she was praying for, and hoped that in the presence of the soldier home from the front, He would listen. She asked Him if it was right to do 'Henry V'. It was a long cast and would need more actors, and that meant spending more money. The last sentence of the prayer was that God should send her some good actors— and as an afterthought she added the word 'cheap'. Now this was not said in any mean spirit. I know that Miss Baylis would have liked to pay her actors big salaries if the money had been her own, but since it belonged to the Vic, she would be careful of every penny. So she prayed to God for good actors—cheap, and her prayer was certainly answered and for some years."

In this same interview, Russell Thorndike remarked that when Lilian Baylis spoke of the Old Vic, her face lit up. This was a dedicated woman, even if the sphere of her dedication may seem a little odd to some of us. She told the soldier to whom she was speaking that she believed in Love and God, and that without Love and God she could not possibly run her theatre. Like his sister, Russell Thorndike was won for the Vic; and as soon as he became well enough, was taking small parts and assisting in all manner of ways.

Towards the end of Lilian Baylis's career, a girl named Patricia Don Young applied, and was accepted, as a student in the Old Vic Dramatic School. She has left a picture of her experiences in a book called *Dramatic School*. She writes of Miss Baylis with the greatest affection, and of the warm, friendly atmosphere that there was about the school and the theatre. "Love God, work hard, and never let the Old Vic down," she was told in Miss Baylis's lecture to the incoming students. To the latter these youngsters were never anything else than "children". That was the way in which she always spoke of them. Though, says Miss Young, we must often have been a nuisance, noisy, extravagant, inexperienced, "one was rarely made to feel it. Without a doubt, Lilian Baylis's firm Christian grasp of the entire organisation was responsible for much".

It is Russell Thorndike who tells the story which we should like to act as the barb of this particular chapter. It concerns an occasion when the Vic was threatened not with the ordinary kind of crisis which it was always facing and surmounting but, this time, with a demand which threatened its immediate existence. Miss Baylis called a Governor's meeting. She

harangued and pleaded. All was in vain. For the lack of some
hundreds of pounds it seemed that all her work was to go down
in ruins. Left alone within the threatened walls of her theatre,
after the others had gone, "she could not bear it. She had to
get away, even though only for a few hours. She mounted her
bicycle and rode out of London. The exertion, and the sight of
the green fields, began to restore her failing courage. On
the way back she passed a village church and resolved on a new
method. She would not pray for help: she would demand it.
Placing her bike against the churchyard wall, she stalked into
the church, which was empty, save for a cleaner at work.
Straight up the aisle she marched, and into the chancel. Standing in front of the altar she spoke aloud to God. She confessed
afterwards that she was very angry. She told God that she was
not going to kneel down as she had knelt for hours to no avail.
She said that the situation at the Vic was ridiculous, that the
money demanded was essential, and that the Almighty, who
could arrange it so easily, really must do something about it.
She left the church, got once more on her bike, and rode back
to the theatre to find that the miracle had happened. On her
desk was a cheque for the amount demanded. Everyone except
Miss Baylis was very surprised that the miracle had happened.
Miss Baylis knew that it would."

There are several things to notice about this prayer: (1) it
was all of a piece with a faith that was so direct and simple
that some would call it "naïve"; (2) Lilian Baylis expected
answers to prayer; (3) this was not a selfish prayer: it was for
her beloved theatre, and for its service to the "people"; (4) the
prayer chimed with her philosophy and practice, that "God
helps those who help themselves": she had done, and would
continue to do, all *she* could to answer her prayer, and live out
her concern for the Vic; (5) this whole enterprise was one to
which she felt definitely "called", and which she served in
honesty and integrity: the prayer is to be understood against

that background, and (6) this was a prayer of desperation—not asking, but demanding!

It is fascinating to go back to the Bible, and to notice there the audacity with which some of God's people at times address Him. Some of the prayers of Moses are of this order (e.g. Numbers 11: 11 ff., 14: 13 ff.). In the Psalms, in particular, there are a number of prayers of this kind. Men, goaded almost beyond endurance, say some extraordinary things to Him. They reprimand Him. They chide Him. They cry aloud. They even roar at Him! Verses 9–26 of Psalm 44, for instance, rise from a man who rebukes God for failing His people. Psalm 79, written when the land is invaded and despoiled, calls on God to help His people. "You are not being true to yourself," the Psalmist seems to be saying, "you are letting your Covenant people be dishonoured. Rise up! Put this right!" All this is in harmony with the glimpse we have of the lessee of the Old Vic telling God that afternoon, as she dismounts from her bicycle and stalks into the church, exactly what she thinks of Him, and *demanding* of Him that He shall act, now! Those who see in this an exhibition of insolence and bad-temper have not seen yet into the inwardness of what was happening. Different temperaments, and folk of different backgrounds, express themselves differently. What we have been looking at is far more an example of straightforwardness, faith and childlike simplicity.

Of late there has been an emphasis on what might be called a "quietist" approach to prayer. God being who He is, we are told, does not need to be cajoled or besought: the idea of "wrestling with God" in prayer is completely out of favour with this school: the idea of demanding things from God is sub-Christian. Whether this idea be fashionable or not, it is not scriptural. Jesus has far more to say in honour of "importunity" than about "receptivity" or even about "submission". Indeed, prayer is, as P. T. Forsyth expresses it, "an encounter of wills". Our will must be behind our praying. And to be expressed with force and power, wills have to be roused.

As a keen Anglo-Catholic, Lilian Baylis would know of the need for obedience and submission, for depending ever-lastingly upon God's grace, but as a Christian, self-taught at this point, she knew also, in the mood of exasperation, that God honours those who speak up to Him. It is here that this woman has much to say to us about a certain straightforward masculinity which we must hold to in the life of prayer. There is a time to ask, and to go on asking and knocking, if need be. God loves, not the subdued spirit, the docile soul, but the importunate, the vividly-desiring, desperately-concerned man or woman. There is a sense in which the Kingdom of Heaven suffereth violence until now!

12. FRANK LAUBACH

Before they call, I will answer, and while they are yet speaking,
I will hear.

ISAIAH 65: 24

IN THE last chapter it might be said that we have followed
a pointer given to us by Paul Claudel. One aspect of vital
prayer, said he, has to do with striving. Within the bounds
of His intention, God delights to honour the demands of
individual wills. Now, we follow another pointer. We have
noted Claudel's insistence that God speaks to us within the
depths of our nature. Within our lifetime there has been
the greatest interest shown in the existence, and in the character, of those depths within us. Psychologists have been busy
probing the secrets of the "deeper mind". Among the facets
of this study, which have to do with both the "ordinary" and
the "deeper" level of the mind, is that of mind-communication
or "telepathy".

My own interest in the subject was kindled by a book
published some years ago. It did not pretend to examine the
subject scientifically; but it did describe a series of experiments
undertaken by an American novelist, Upton Sinclair, and his
wife in the field of "Mental Radio". As a result, Sinclair
himself was convinced that thought communication was
possible between two people "in tune" with one another,
without the use of any media that involved the five senses.

108

All of us have instances of what we call "hunches", thought communications, that have come to us at times involving something of this character. I know of two friends so closely in tune that their letters to one another invariably cross! Evidence concerning these matters is now being carefully collated and scientifically examined.[1]

In the late nineteen-thirties a book entitled *Thoughts through Space* was written by Sherman and Wilkins. Wilkins was a member of the American expedition that went in search of the Soviet airmen lost in the Arctic in the winter of 1937–8. Before he went, his friend and he agreed on an experiment that they would undertake together. Sherman, in his study in New York, would set down the impressions that came to him at agreed times when he understood that Wilkins would be endeavouring, across those intervening miles of space, to communicate with him. To do this he tried to get into a suitably relaxed frame of mind, and to find himself *en rapport* with his friend.

After the session, he would send his notes to a third party, who received from Wilkins information concerning what he had been trying to communicate in this way. The book is a record of these exchanges. Sometimes Sherman "received" nothing at all. Sometimes he seems to have gathered, in quite a remarkable way, what it was that Wilkins was sending out towards him. At other times he is completely wide of the mark. There were still others—and these results are possibly amongst the most interesting of all—when the message seems to have been completely inverted. The subconscious mind can play tricks of this kind. The point of the message seems to have been turned upside down, or inside out. Sherman "got it", but the wrong way round!

Many ingenious theories have been put forward to explain what this phenomenon of telepathy really involves. The plain

[1] G. M. Tyrrell in his Pelican Book on *The Personality of Man* has a chapter setting forth some of the facts as they are being established.

fact seems to be that it is something which exists in its own right, and it is not therefore completely explicable by anything else. It is not, for instance, an explanation but a pictorial hypothesis when the suggestion is made that at the deeper level of the mind we are all linked in a "great universal sea of mind-stuff, in which every individual can be thought of as a wave". According to the terms of this picture, the idea is that contact is possible between one wave and another, because of the common participation in the ground life of the ocean. All we can say at the moment is that, in fortuitous circumstances, it is possible for one mind to communicate with another without material means.

There are two things which this phenomenon seems to say to us about prayer: (1) It reminds us that prayer itself is best understood and thought of as "mind communication". In this case we are trying to make communication between our minds and the Great Mind of God. It reminds us, then, most potently, that what really counts in this realm are not our words, or the things that we pretend to, but our real thoughts. These are what we communicate to God. (2) Telepathy, perhaps, enables us to understand a little better what it is we are doing when we endeavour to help others through our prayers. The world-famous Dr. Frank C. Laubach is very interested to make this point.

In *Prayer: The Mightiest Force in the World*, he reminds us, for example, of Christ's words in Rev. 3: 20: "Behold, I stand at the door and knock . . ." But, says Laubach, the door is closed in all too many cases, and the key is lost. So many of our contemporaries never talk to God, never think about Him. Now, if we pray for a man a thousand miles away, or for the man next door (for in this realm, as in that of telepathy, distance matters nothing) at the moment of our praying, his deeper mind may be in tune with ours. Our prayer, as it goes out, is used by God and, reinforced and redirected, may help the other man to open the door of his heart. It may start in him a desire for God. Desire is what tunes men in to God. Our prayer then may help to make a man accessible to God: changing the analogy, we can say that we can perform the service of the switchboard operator in a telephone exchange, and help to put him through to God!

Imagine, at this moment, that, in various places, a hundred people are praying for the Prime Minister, or for the leader of the Soviet Union. Deep in the other man's mind, at this identical time, there may be the stirring of a sense of need. Our prayer may vitally reinforce that, and aid a desire to look to God (or, if the phraseology will not fit a Communist, a Higher Power) for help and inspiration to solve some pressing problem. It is true that we cannot, in this way, force another man to think or act against his will: but it is given to us to bring the thought of God, and the power of God, near. Our vicarious faith may enable him, for himself, to come to a moment of openness and faith.

It is important that no one must misunderstand what we are saying: prayer operates at a deeper level than telepathy as ordinarily described. We are using it as an analogy, as a way of understanding what we do, or can do, in praying for one another. Prayer is *not* communication between our human minds, on the ordinary level. It is uttered *to* God and *in* God; and in this conscious communion with Him we are given the glorious privilege of bringing His forces to bear upon the needs of others. It is here that there lies the possibility of our co-operation.

Dr. Frank C. Laubach, an American Presbyterian minister, a man of most original mind, likes to think of prayer after this fashion. Laubach[1] himself is a world-renowned figure: the

---

[1] One of Dr. Laubach's latest books, *The Master Speaks*, is an original and inspired approach to our Lord's life. Published by Arthur James (Evesham).

prime mover in the "World Literacy Campaign", having evolved a method by which illiterate adults can swiftly learn to read and write in their own tongue. Under his leadership, this liberation into the world of literacy must have come to thousands of backward peoples in all parts of the world: in Asia, Africa, and America. His method is now in use, to my certain knowledge, in over ninety languages. And Frank Laubach will be the first to tell you that this whole movement has grown, and has been baptized since its inception, in prayer: his own prayers and those of others whom he has enlisted in the same concern for those imprisoned in illiteracy.

It is a fascinating story to discover how this campaign started. In 1915 Laubach, accompanied by his wife, went to the Philippines. For the first seven years of missionary service, he built up a series of evangelical churches on the North Coast of Mindanao, and, travelling about the islands, got to know something of their peoples and their varied needs.

One of his concerns was to see the new Union Theological Seminary set up in Manila. He took a major share in the planning for its establishment. In *Everyman's Adventure*, Dr. Rebecca Beard says that Laubach hoped to become its president. He lost that appointment, by a single vote. "He was greatly disappointed," she reports. "He almost felt that he could not face another audience. It so weighed upon him that his health began to suffer. Then one day he utterly abandoned his former ambition and relinquished his longing and desire for high position. He gave himself absolutely and completely to the Father and started practising the presence of God every minute of his life. He was led to go down amongst the illiterate native people and serve them. God took Frank Laubach's yearning and his relinquishment and gave him a great idea. There were given to him a plan and a message whereby he could teach illiterate backward people to read, and to bring Christianity into their lives. Had he won the seminary appointment in Manila, Frank Laubach's name might never have been known round the world as it is today. Through relinquishment, his greater destiny is being fulfilled."

It was amongst the Mohamedan Moros on Mindanao that Laubach first worked this out. In 1930, when he went to them, they were a wild people, almost entirely illiterate, and completely at enmity with their Christian neighbours, the Filipinos. Laubach was able to break down this enmity, and within a few years, 45,000 of the Moros living round the lake could read and write! Readers of his *Letters of a Modern Mystic* will know the inside story of this. He himself as he began his work amongst them—after his fierce disappointment, remember—planned to live "filling every minute full of the thought of God", and to "line up his actions with the will of God".

"I feel simply carried along each hour, doing my part in a plan which is far beyond myself," he wrote in a letter to his father on January 29th, 1930. "This sense of co-operation with God in little things is what so astonishes me, for I have never felt it this way before."

On March 1st he wrote: "The sense of being led by an unseen hand which takes mine while another hand reaches ahead and prepares the way, grows upon me daily. I do not need to strain at all to find opportunity. It piles in upon me as the waves roll over the beach . . ." Out of his initial disappointment and frustration came this tremendous sense of opportunity and adventure, involving a whole new realm of service.

It is also important for us to notice Laubach's testimony to the way in which he has felt the support of other people's prayers during the Literacy Campaign as it has grown and developed. He speaks of times when he has felt a wave of encouragement and a new sense of fervour coming to him. He says he is certain that those were times when many of his friends and well-wishers were remembering him and his work in their prayers. The "telepathy" of prayer was something which he himself was experiencing. Days or weeks after such an occasion, he tells us, he has received a letter, saying, "We were praying for you—did you feel it?" Often he could reply, "Yes, and it made everything better."

Laubach is a man with some deep concerns on his mind. One is that we, in the Western nations, shall learn swiftly, while there is time, how the privileged peoples of the world can help the underprivileged: "What constantly surprised me," he writes, "is the amazing ease with which a little unselfish service conquers people's hearts if we discover what they want and then give it to them humbly and unselfishly. One of the most urgent needs in the world is for the three-fifths of the human race who are illiterate to learn to read. They feel like blind people, or like men in prison; and when we teach them to read, sitting down beside them like friends, and loving them and praying for them, they melt at once and are as grateful as a blind man when the cataracts are cut from his eyes."

Another concern of his is to mobilise the forces of prayer. He wants a volume of prayer to be directed towards such agencies as the United Nations, and all its organisations: to the rulers of the nations, and particularly towards the peoples and rulers of nations from whom, at this moment, we are divided. In *Channels of Spiritual Power*, he declares, "We Christians do not dream what power we have. We are committing a terrible sin against the world in failing to use it." We should pray for labour leaders, trades union officials, statesmen. We should pray for that backward three-fifths of the human race, and for the people who are trying to help them.

And how shall we pray for them? It is here that we return to the analogy with which we began. The most useful service we can do for anybody, says Laubach, is to link him with God. Our prayers to do this need not be long prayers. Laubach is a great advocate of the "flash prayer", made whenever the thought of somebody else comes to mind: linking him immediately with the thought of God!

Prayer is the great connecting agency: as swift as electricity it is through to God. Our human mind is in living touch with Him. By thinking of others in this vital way—linking the thought of God with the thought of the other person—we shall be doing far more for him than we know. "In that instant," says Laubach, "you have built a bridge of thought between him and God. We who do this habitually are convinced that it is a very potent power. The results are far above our expectations."

13. JACK WINSLOW

Prayer for Guidance

And thine ears shall hear a word behind thee, saying, This is the way, walk ye in it, when ye turn to the right hand, and when ye turn to the left.

ISAIAH 30: 21

THE THREE great influences, says Jack Winslow, which have strongly affected his experience of prayer are (1) his upbringing at home, and his experiences in John R. Mott's Mission at Oxford when he was a young man; (2) then, the twenty years spent in India (it is remarkable, by the way, looking over the chapters of this book to notice how many of the people of whom we have written pay a similar tribute to India), and (3) contact with the Oxford Group, from whom he gained a special insight into the "prayer of attention"—or, as we shall describe it, how to wait on God for definite guidance in the immediate affairs of one's daily living.

Jack Winslow has written an enthralling autobiography covering his varied career, as a boy at Eton, an undergraduate at Oxford, a curate in Wimbledon, a missionary in India, a chaplain at Bryanston School, and then co-founder and chaplain of the great experiment in fellowship and Christian adventuring at Lee Abbey in Dorset. He entitles it *Eyelids of the Dawn.*

It is interesting to note, before we draw away from the subject of the last chapter, that in that autobiography Jack Winslow tells of a time in India when he tried an experiment in telepathy. He was to conduct a service on the following day. Too late in the evening to do anything about it, he suddenly became aware that they lacked the necessary communion wine. The only hope, from that remote area where they were, was to try to make an Indian padre, who would be joining them in the morning "telepathically" aware of the deficiency. He, and the members of the group assembled with him, agreed to attempt this. Before they went to sleep, they thought of their friend at Headquarters, and tried to "get into touch" with his "unconscious mind" as he might be sleeping, or preparing for bed. Sure enough, the man's first thought on waking was, "I wonder if those people have enough wine. I must be ready with some more"! Winslow comments that he, too, finds that the concept of telepathy has given him a fresh understanding of the possibilities of intercessory prayer. Indeed, it would be possible to go back over all the past chapters in turn, and find in the life of this man illustrations that would fit the subject matter of each of them. A friend of his says that he especially thinks of him as "a living repository of the prayers of all the ages": he means by this that Jack Winslow is steeped in the literature of prayer and concerning prayer, and knows, and uses, in a way that is quite remarkable, the great prayers that have come down to us from the past. But our special concern here is to note what he has to say to us about prayer and guidance, and to observe how he came to make his own discoveries in this connection.

During his years—the early years of the century—at Balliol College, Oxford, John R. Mott conducted a mission in the University. What impressed our particular undergraduate most was Mott's stress on the importance of what he called the "Morning Watch". Every day, he said, should start with an unhurried period of prayer and meditation. Jack Winslow took the advice and since, as he explains in the booklet *When I Awake*, he has never ceased recommending this practice to other people. He claims that for him it has been an "ever

117

fresh spring of power". Later, when he was a curate in Wimbledon, a Missioner at an open-air service was talking about prayer. For a moment or two the racket of a passing tram drowned the speaker's voice. As the tram sped into the distance, the Missioner pointed to it and said, "Look! How swiftly and easily it travels with its arm lifted to the live wire above! And how powerless it would be to move an inch without that vital contact." The "Morning Watch", so Winslow found, was just such a vital contact with the everlasting source of power.

India's special insistence concerned the deepening of these habits of quiet meditation, already begun under the influence of John R. Mott and others. Jack Winslow says that this call to quiet meditation is outstanding amongst the best gifts that India can pass on to the Western world. In India, too, Winslow found himself sympathising with the Indian struggle for Home Rule, and for a freer expression of the native Indian genius at all points—inside Church life, as well as outside it.

Narayan Vaman Tilak became one of his friends. One of Tilak's poems, breathing the very spirit of the man, has been translated by Nicol Macnicol, and appears now in a number of Western hymn books:

> One who is all unfit to count
> As scholar in Thy school,
> Thou of Thy love hast named a friend—
> O kindness wonderful!

> So weak am I, O gracious Lord,
> So all unworthy Thee,
> That e'en the dust upon Thy feet
> Outweighs me utterly.

> Thou dwellest in unshadowed light,
> All sin and shame above—
> That Thou shouldst bear our sin and shame,
> How can I tell such love?

Ah, did not He the heavenly throne
A little thing esteem,
And not unworthy for my sake
A mortal body deem?

When in His flesh they drove the nails,
Did He not all endure?
What name is there to fit a life
So patient and so pure?

So, Love itself in human form,
For love of me He came;
I cannot look upon His face
For shame, for bitter shame.

If there is aught of worth in me,
It comes from Thee alone;
Then keep me safe, for so, O Lord,
Thou keepest but Thine own.

Another strong influence was that of C. F. Andrews, of whom we shall be writing in the next chapter. The way that Andrews identified himself with India and the Indians affected Jack Winslow very greatly. For long the latter had felt the difficulty of trying to reach Indians, while yet maintaining the standards of the West in behaviour and dress. Andrews' example seemed to supply the answer. "I thank God," writes Winslow, "for the friendship, during thirty years, of Charlie Andrews. To be with him was a benediction, for his whole being radiated love. It was this man's life and writings which first kindled my desire to enter more deeply into the spirit of India and to be more closely identified with her people."

Thus it was that Jack Winslow was concerned that more typically Indian methods should be found to present Christ to India's people. Whilst musing on these matters, an experience came to him, an answer to the prayers and thoughts of many months past, which he regards as "divine guidance".

It was on August 12th, 1919—the date can be pin-pointed—whilst he was on furlough in England. He had been reading an account of the ancient Ashrams of India. The sages would select a place beside a river, or on some hilltop, whose natural beauty helped forward the spirit of meditation, and there they would gather their disciples into an ashram, training them in the ways of religion, and then sending them out to teach others.

The thought came to Jack Winslow—why not adapt this idea to Christian use? It was a method already being revived in modern India—Gandhi and Tagore both had ashrams. But what came to him in that flash was not just an idea: he *saw* the picture of a Christian ashram, complete in all its details. And it was on the basis of what he then saw and noted down that he worked for many years. Others, too, were awake to this vision. In 1920, Winslow and a group of young Indians began to live together in community in an ashram the equivalent of whose name would be "The Society of Servants belonging to Christ". It was thus that the Christian ashram movement was launched in India—a movement which has had repercussions throughout the world, and in India itself, as Stanley Jones has made clear, has helped enormously to make known to that country the *Christ of the Indian Road*.

In September 1932, whilst leading a Convention at Jaffna in Ceylon, another "milestone" experience occurred. Winslow had been hearing from many of his friends about a new sense of liberation they had experienced through contact with the movement then known as The Oxford Group. In the train coming to the Convention he had himself been reading A. J. Russell's book about the Group, *For Sinners Only*. Doubtless, the Group's standards of absolute honesty, love, and unselfishness had already made an impression on him, as well as its insistence upon the value of frank confession and witness. On the fifth day of the Convention, when it seemed right to ask for definite decisions for Christ, in the silence before making this appeal, there came to Winslow an unmistakable sense of guidance. It was that he himself should tell the congregation of his own need, then and there, to make a deeper surrender of his own life, and to mention some of the things which he now knew had been obstructing him from doing that. The results of this step were, he says, astonishing. The harvest that came in the Convention itself deserved that adjective. Quietly, and without undue emotion, the hundreds who committed themselves to Christ were shepherded. Next morning, Winslow tells how he awoke "to a new world, with a sense of having been re-made. New life had flowed into me". The most significant thing of all that he experienced was, he says, "a new outgoing love for people. . . . It was sheer miracle".

Following this there came closer contact with the Group and its leaders. In the kind of fellowship that it fostered in those early days, and in the atmosphere of changed lives amidst which it lived, it seemed to Winslow that they were back in the Acts of the Apostles.

In 1944, Jack Winslow went for the first time to Lee Abbey, with which place, I suppose, his name will always be associated. This great house stands west of Lynton in a cleft of the rugged North Devonshire coast. At that time it was being used as a Preparatory School evacuated to a place of safety. Roger de Pemberton had secured the use of it during the summer holidays for a House Party for folk from the churches of Rochester. The experiences in which Jack Winslow shared during those days of mingled holiday and Christian fellowship clinched in him and some of the others a feeling that they had all had—that there was a need for just such a place where people could "come apart" and enjoy refreshment of mind, body and spirit; and where the life of the Church itself could be revitalised. As they talked and prayed on that spot, it seemed that Lee Abbey was the very place for this experiment.

Acting on the conviction that "where God guides, He

provides", they went ahead with arrangements to buy Lee Abbey when the war ended and the school returned to its own home. The total expense of purchase and re-adaptation was about £40,000—which represented an enormous venture of faith for the body of Trustees that was formed. Jack Winslow records that, by the time of writing his autobiography, only £10,000 remained of that original indebtedness. Meanwhile, some 3,500 guests attend the place annually, and the amount of good that it has seen accomplished in changed lives, deepened spirituality, new-found understanding, recovered faith and zeal, is incalculable. Lee Abbey must be reckoned amongst the most alive forces in the Church of England in this country at the moment.

"If and when God wills," Winslow says, "He can send us sudden and unexpected directions, coming on us like a bolt from the blue." He has found it like that in his own experience. These are swift, intuitive ideas and commands, coming in a moment, completely unexpected, and often apparently unsought. But Jack Winslow also knows, and stresses, the value of the "prayer of attention", and has experienced for many years the sense of intimate, daily guidance which this brings. It is, indeed, sustained prayer of this kind that attunes us to those sudden bursts of guidance, and enables us to know whether we are dealing with something emanating from our own imagination, or whether what we are hearing is "the voice of God". We have trained ourselves to listen to that voice.

Guidance like this does not come to those who are not already surrendered and committed, willing and ready to be used, and already engaged in service for the Kingdom. All these things are pre-requisites. When we have proved ourselves ready and willing, and if we lay ourselves open to it, we can reckon that guidance will reach us: on some occasions it may be of specific character—a reminder of someone to see, a letter to write, a long-overlooked debt to repay. Guidance may also come in the realm of ideas. We may suddenly see—and know that God is guiding us so to do—right into the heart of some problem that has long perplexed us.

The fact is that most of us, in our praying, devote far less time and attention to "waiting upon God"—to the listening side of prayer—than we devote to the incessantly active and vocal form of praying that most of us indulge in. "We ought," says Jack Winslow, "to give more time to listening to God than we do to speaking to Him." How many of us do that? He says that it is his own practice to listen to God's orders for the day ahead: these orders are taken seriously, and in his "Morning Watch" Winslow notes down the thoughts that come concerning details to be attended to—letters to be written, things to be said, folk to be seen, etc. Listening in this way, and following out the orders as they come have given him, he declares, an entirely new sense of his "individual part in God's plan".

HORIZONS BEFORE US

14. C. F. ANDREWS

SOCIAL CONCERN

Deliver us from evil.
MATTHEW 6: 13

WHEN READING some words of John S. Hoyland, I knew that I must bring the name of C. F. Andrews into this galaxy of prayer explorers. I had thought of doing this before, since Andrews has written so beautifully of *The Inner Life*, *Christ in the Silence*, and *Christ and Prayer*. My thought then was of the contrast between his words about peace and the need for the quietness and stillness of prayer and our noisy and distracted manner of living in the Western world. My immediate thought of Andrews himself has always been one of "saintliness". Many years ago, when I was a theological student, I saw him and heard him speak. With his flowing beard and beautiful face, he reminded one of the impression one carries at the back of one's mind of what the figure of Christ must have looked like. Of C. F. Andrews I know it to be literally true that one knew when this man entered a room, even if one had one's back to the door and had not seen him enter.

Hoyland's words, however, made me realise that I must write of Andrews in a way that might, at the outset, seem to be utterly different. By his life, by his prayers, this man accomplished marvels in the difficult sphere of human relations. He struck a blow at embattled forces of evil. He was a "fighting saint".

Here are the words which reminded me of this element in the story of C.F.A. ("Christ's Faithful Apostle" as an Indian once so rightly named him). They are from *Prayer and the Social Revolution*: "In the past such apparently impregnable strongholds of arrogance and wrong have vanished almost in a night. The soul has gone out of them, as the soul went out of the Slave Trade, or the Gladiatorial Games, or the Indenture System for Indian labourers, as soon as the will of one human being, a John Woolman, a Telemachus, a Charles Andrews, was given wholeheartedly to God for the answering of the prayer 'Deliver us from evil'. No power on earth, however formidable, can stand against really Christian prayer, backed by really Christian consecration even of one soul." I want us to think of one whose life and prayer together echoed as well as answered the prayer "Deliver us from evil", and who saw the answer being achieved in terms of changed, and changing, circumstances.

Andrews wrote his autobiography, and characteristically entitled it, *What I Owe to Christ*. In it he described his conversion, which happened when he was about to go to Cambridge. In his "Irvingite" Church, of which his father was minister, no stress had been laid upon conversion as a necessary step in the Christian life: but Andrews' own experience, without the preconditioning, followed the Pauline and Augustinian pattern. After some hours of struggle in his own room, when a sense of peace and forgiveness flooded his soul, deep anguish at the thought of his own sinfulness and need was ended. He knew, without any doubt, that Christ was His Saviour and Lord. Andrews himself said that all his future life was lived against the background of that experience, and the new relationship into which it brought him.

Within a day or two, Andrews found himself doing something undreamt of before: near his church was a slum; into this area the new-born Christian went, restrained instinctively, as he tells us, from talking overmuch about his new-found experience, but making friends and seeking to help as need arose and as folk would allow him.

It was not until he was thirty-three years of age that he went to India as a missionary. In the interval he had left his father's church, and was now an ordained clergyman in the Church of England, having served in poverty-stricken Monkwearmouth, and in the Pembroke College mission in Walworth, finally returning as a don to Cambridge. The step of becoming a missionary was of such a character and, on reaching India, involved him in such a mental and spiritual upheaval that he always spoke of the beginning of his life in that country as a "second birthday". He was, so he declared, one of the "twice-born" (though one wonders whether, in this context, the expression should not be, "thrice-born"!).

Indian life itself, and the people he met in India, conspired to deepen his interest in prayer, and to encourage him to spend more time in it. He tells us this in the first few pages of *The Inner Life*. Hitherto, the necessity of "getting things done" had filled his mind: "The work that had to be done among the poor and oppressed for His sake had so filled my mind and occupied my attention that I had begun to grudge every moment of the day that was not spent on active service." He had to learn "to study to be quiet". The change of environment made him realise how "unbalanced" his life had been. Through these periods of quiet and meditation into which he was now able to enter came power to do things really effectively.

For a variety of reasons, in 1914 Andrews took a step which he called "the greatest break in my whole life". In order to do his work in India in a way that would be unencumbered, he left the Anglican ministry. So that he might go the full way with this radical step, he also "gave away his life's savings and became a wanderer". Hoyland's book on C. F. Andrews tells us this, and adds, "I do not think any of his friends knew how Charlie was supported during those strenuous years. . . . He certainly lived on the barest minimum both during the anti-indenture struggle and afterwards." He, too, was one who believed that Christ would see to the necessities of His own who were endeavouring to accomplish His purposes.

The indenture system, whose abuses so moved Andrews, was one under which labour was recruited in India and shipped, under what proved to be almost conditions of slavery, to Natal, Fiji, the West Indies, British Guiana and other places where cheap labour was wanted under tropical conditions. "Everywhere," as Andrews himself rightly said about this system, "it reproduced many of the old evils of slavery in an exaggerated form." In South Africa, with racial prejudice already inflamed, the position of the Indians was tragic indeed. Here Andrews met Mahatma Gandhi, who was working for his fellow-Indians, and suffering for them too. Both men strongly influenced each other.

There is a fascinating picture which Andrews has left us of the kind of thoughts that moved in his mind as, at Pretoria, he waited with Gandhi in the hope of seeing General Smuts and interesting him in the campaign for justice for the Indians. "Often," he says, "I would get up very early in the silence before the dawn and sit still for hours, pondering over the meaning of human life and its brief history on this planet— so insignificant yet so infinitely great; a moment of consciousness rising out of the inanimate void to sink back into the inanimate again. Yet all the more it seemed vitally important to employ every speck of it in God's service, with Christ to guide and direct me."

In 1915 Andrews, staying at Santiniketan with Rabindranath Tagore, was stricken with cholera. Tagore, at great risk to himself, nursed him through this terrible illness. While recovering, Andrews picked up a Blue Book on indentured Indian labour. Glancing through its pages he read of the appalling suicide rate amongst indentured Indians in Fiji. The misery of the Indians there seemed far worse than that in Natal, which he had already seen for himself.

Soon after this, lying on his couch at midday, he saw a vision of a poor Indian labourer whom he had met in Natal, with torn back, bruised and bleeding, who had, however, shrunk away from him when he learned that the one offering help was an Englishman. This time, the man was looking at him most piteously. "As I watched him with great sorrow," writes Andrews, "his face changed and I saw instead the face of Jesus, the Good Shepherd. . . . The image was so clear that my whole heart went out in reverence and worship. As I lay back there, it was some time after the vision had faded before I realised that it had been a waking dream, created by my own intense imagination and objectively thrown outside of me by my subconscious mind."

But, having seen the vision, Andrews now knew where his path lay. How it could happen he did not know. He was still dreadfully weak from his attack of fever. But the gathering concern and desire of those days helped forward his recovery. The report, which he published on his return, of the awful conditions in Fiji led to the passing of an act abolishing the system. Unfortunately, a clause about "delay being needed" in order to bring about "the necessary adjustments" made it virtually ineffective. It was after such hard work, struggle and prayer that, on January 1st, 1920, indenture was definitely and finally abolished not only in Fiji, but throughout the whole of the British Colonies. That this was brought about is in no small measure due to the sympathy, prayer and unstinted sacrifice of this one man—C. F. Andrews.

Belief and action, prayer and deed were inseparably connected in his life. So far from being an impractical dreamer, a sentimental seeker of quiet, a mystic and a poet removed from the world of men, this man who in India learned the secret of peace and who customarily spent many hours in meditation and prayer, achieved what men of action had been unable to accomplish. After his death, one of the tributes paid to him mentioned this aspect of his life: "On the surface it seemed as if the gentle sentimentalist had little chance of bargaining with hard-boiled industrialists and matter-of-fact officials, but when they met it was the prophet in homespun who was fit to get the better of the men of the world."

"Charlie Andrews was simple like a child," wrote Mahatma Gandhi of him, "upright as a die and shy to a degree." His was the "simplicity that is toward Christ", the simplicity of the child who is of the Kingdom of Heaven. In his journeys throughout the world—made chiefly on behalf of some group of suffering people, such as the indentured Indian labourers— he was distressed by the trust that he saw everywhere people were putting in riches. Materialism, it seemed to him, was choking the life of the spirit in man. "In Australia and New Zealand, and more still in America," he writes, "I found that the rapid increase of material things had so forced up the rate of living to its highest point, that simplicity had become regarded as of little value." By his words and still more by the manner of his life, Andrews was always reminding people of the treasures that come only to those who are childlike, "poor in spirit", looking for the way of Christ.

"Now that I have reached old age," he said to a group of young Indian Christians, towards the end of his life, "believe me when I say that this love of Christ in the heart is the truest and best and greatest treasure that anyone can possibly find in this life of ours." Let us be active, he told them, in all manner of ways, and find Christ in our work: but, more than that, let us find Him in silence "in the inner chamber of our hearts, when we are praying and are all alone. And if we find Him thus, both in action and in rest, we shall indeed win the victory."

John Ellerton, thinking doubtless most of all of work at "the loom, the forge, the mart" wrote:

> Work shall be prayer, if all be wrought
> As Thou wouldst have it done;
> And prayer, by Thee inspired and taught
> Itself with work be one.

This is what we shall note especially concerning C. F. Andrews's praying—it was an expression of his Christian integrity. He who was "Christ's Faithful Apostle" made of his work and his prayer one thing. Prayer drew him into the battle against evil, both in the secret place, and in the market place. By this he won his victories for others in the social struggle. He had the "simplicity which is towards Christ". His was an integrated life, and his prayer had the support of a supreme personal honesty.

15. FORBES ROBINSON AND OTHERS

PRAYING FOR OTHERS

Pray one for another.

JAMES 5: 16

A NUMBER of people are fortunate enough to possess a copy of the privately printed *Letters to His Friends* by Forbes Robinson. Robinson was a shy man, who spent most of his time in the precincts of Cambridge colleges. He died in 1904 at the age of thirty-six, a don and an ordained clergyman of the Church of England. As readers of the *Letters* will know, he had a remarkable influence on a number of Cambridge undergraduates and on a circle of friends who, through him, came to share in the same kind of vital and winsome Christianity that he knew.

The fascinating thing is that discerning people report that the centre of Forbes Robinson's influence was his praying. Behind his talks and contacts with the folk whom he influenced there was always this background. He himself thought prayer to be the paramount force in any attempt to influence others for Christ.

An intimate friend tells of a conversation he had with him towards the end of his life. The friend had begun to realise that much of Robinson's spiritual power was connected with his praying. On this occasion they were talking, in the strictest confidence, about these matters. Robinson confessed that in his earlier years he had taken every chance of appealing personally to men to offer themselves to Christ. "As I grow older," he went on to say, "I become more diffident, and now often, when I desire to see the Truth come home to any man, I say to myself, 'If I have him here he will spend half an hour with me. Instead I will spend that half an hour in prayer for him.'"

To another friend he wrote this: "We shall not have to talk so much to others if we pray more for them. We talk and we do not influence, or we influence only for a time, because our lives are not more prayer-full."

"My idea of friendship is prayer," was another of his remarks. To illustrate this, let us look at a letter written to "G.J.C." in 1900, someone who had evidently just been drawn into the circle: "When I call a man by his Christian name, I usually make it a rule to pray for him. I shall do so in your case. I will try to pray every day. I wonder whether you would sometimes pray for me: I believe immensely in the power of prayer."

If anyone spoke to him of a friend who was proving difficult and disappointing to win for Christ, the advice he would receive from Robinson would be: "Pray for him, believe in him: believe in him, pray for him." Here was a man who would not give up his hope for others lightly. Again and again someone of the most unlikely type was won for Christ, or someone who had slipped away was recovered; and a factor of the highest importance in the situation was the power and persistence of Forbes Robinson's praying for him.

Without doubt, too, Robinson himself grew in stature, and in power, through this steady, selfless praying. The Rev. Digby Kittermaster, who knew him intimately, wrote, "Men must sometimes—with all reverence be it said—have experienced in his presence the same kind of a feeling of some great unseen influence at work as that which the disciples must have experienced in the presence of Christ after He, apart and alone, had watched through the night with God in prayer. For many an hour of his life did Forbes spend like that, striving with God for those he loved."

In the collection of *Letters*, there are some written to a young clergyman whose initials are D.B.K. In the first of these he gives such wise advice to the new curate as that he should maintain a wide circle of friends and not associate only with parsons. He goes on to stress the value of prayer for individual people: "to influence you must love," he writes, "to love, you must pray." He tells D.B.K. something of the greatest value: that the way to love a person is to pray for him, and that praying for another always leads to a deepened interest in, and sympathy for, him.

"Just try to pray for some one person committed to your charge—say for half an hour or an hour—and you will begin really to love him. As you lay his life before God, as you think of his needs and hopes and failings and possibilities, as you pray earnestly for him as you would for some one whom you feel intense affection for; at the end of the time you will feel more interested in him. . . . You will not, it may be, have time to pray for many in this way, but you will learn imperceptibly to extend your sympathy—to feel real love for many more."

Eighteen months later, in another letter, Robinson returns to this theme of going out of ourselves in love and prayer and concern for others: "Each time we go out of self, and enter into another 'ego'," he tells D.B.K., "we return the richer for our sacrifice. We take up other lives into our own, and are richer than a millionaire. I think that when the other 'ego' is most unlike our own—when at first sight the man is repulsive, and (worse still) uninteresting to us—when the sacrifice is great, if we would see life through his eyes, share his ambitions, fears, longings and mental outlook, then is the time when we are peculiarly rewarded for our pains. Our consciousness is larger, more human, more divine than before. . . .

But pray. You enter then into another man's 'ego'. . . . Your influence, your life, your all, depends on prayer."

General Gordon, a man of different type and calling from Robinson, witnesses to so many of the same discoveries in his own life. He was a man of unique power, and a study of his life reveals that much of this was due to habits of steady and persistent prayer. It was his custom always before meeting anyone, be he rebel chief or enemy, to pray for him. In this way, Gordon believed, he established an invisible link with him. There are some astonishing stories of his influence over others, and of visits paid, almost unescorted, into the camp of slave-traders and enemies, from which he returned unscathed.

Gordon kept a long list of people for whom he prayed. In a letter quoted in Lord Elton's recent biography, Gordon confides this to a certain Mrs. Freese: "Do you know, my experience is that if you pray for anyone, that person is sure to like you, let him be ever so much against you at the beginning, at any rate, he will be drawn to you, and eventually his path in life will cross your own. It is even in a worldly way a good investment."

Pastor Niemöller has been telling congregations in this country recently of the experiences he underwent in prison and concentration camp as a result of his outspoken condemnation of the Nazi persecution of the Jews. He spent eight years in solitary confinement, and for a long time had a cell which had full sight of the gallows. As he watched many being executed, it seemed inevitable that his turn would come; and he fell to thinking what he would do if his feet ever took him up those steps which he had seen so many others climb. He decided that he would turn on his captors and say, "It is you who should be here. Not me. It is you who have committed irreparable wrongs. You have slaughtered men like this. You ought to die. Not me." But the more he thought, the more he knew that this was not Christ's way. He loved His enemies, and prayed for those who put Him to death. Until I can show that spirit, Niemöller said to himself, I am not worthy of His love. Gradually he came to know the meaning of loving one's enemies. In as hard a school as any, he had to learn this, and began to pray for his captors. He, too, says that his thoughts for them, and about them, imperceptibly began to change.

Praying for others is seen at the utmost reach of selfless concern when it is for one's enemies. It is from the Lord that we learn this kind of praying, and by His Love within us that we are able to carry it through.

Niemöller also experienced the power of prayer in the reverse direction—as one who knew himself prayed for—and he has told us what strength he gained from that. There came a time when the senselessness and injustice of his imprisonment so burdened his mind that he was utterly depressed. His father, then aged eighty, was allowed to visit him. As he was leaving the concentration camp, he put his hand on his son's shoulder and said, "My boy, remember that the Icelanders, the Esquimaux—the whole Christian Church—is praying for you." What heart that knowledge put into him! In the days that followed his depression vanished. It *was* true that others were praying for him. He continued to feel a remarkable sense of invisible support.

It is humbling, and wonderfully strengthening, to know that one is remembered in the prayers of other people. It is glorious to be much engaged in helpful, positive praying for others. The miracle of Christ has happened in us when that praying is actually for those who have been showing themselves to be our enemies. The power is at work by which enemies can be turned to friends.

Do you remember the verse in Job 42: 10 that reports that "The Lord turned the captivity of Job when he prayed for his friends; also the Lord gave Job twice as much as he had before"? Surely there is something here which the writer of that Old Testament work would have us discover: something which he himself must have experienced at first-hand. Job had argued with God, stormed at him because of the injustice done to him. He had uttered cries, prayers, petitions. None of these had availed to "turn his captivity". The laws of prayer at which we are looking emphasise not only that "negative" praying is a mistake, but show that merely self-concerned prayer is on a very low level, too. Coué's *Law of Reversed Effort* is a psychological law which just as surely shows itself at work in the realm of prayer. By praying about our troubles we are often merely aggravating them instead of praying them away. It is when we get our attention *off ourselves* that God's love and power can flow into us unimpeded.

In the North-east of England lives a great friend of mine, a retired Methodist minister. For years he was Secretary of the British and Foreign Bible Society in the three northernmost countries. Now, aged over eighty, he and his wife, who is some seven years younger, exercise a unique ministry of personal help to a host of people. Prayer lies at the heart of this. It provides the explanation of how the two of them have been enabled to give almost miraculous guidance to people bewildered and puzzled by their circumstances and to steady folk in the deepest of trouble. By this power at work, for example, a would-be suicide had been turned to a contributing and creative member of society.

Over the years Tom and Florence have come to feel that, for them, intercession is the crowning ministry of their lives. Gradually a pattern and a method have taken shape. At six o'clock every morning, so they tell us, they wake without any difficulty. A cup of tea is ready, prepared. Over this cup of tea, they share whatever of relevant interest is on their minds. Then, almost always their time of prayer begins with the collect:

Almighty God, unto whom all hearts are open, all desires known, and from whom no secrets are hid; cleanse the thoughts of our hearts by the inspiration of Thy Holy Spirit, that we may perfectly love Thee, and worthily magnify Thy Holy Name, through Jesus Christ our Lord. Amen.

This prayer, says Tom, is the perfect prayer for their purpose, preparing them for inward communion. They are able to remain in that communion as they bring their petitions and think of individual people. First they pray for the members of their own family, which is quite a large one, including a score of homes and three generations! Then, for their "spiritual family", which is much larger still, including folk in all the churches, folk at home and missionaries overseas. Then comes special thought for those "on the threshold of the spiritual family". Then "the living Church throughout the world", with special mention of particular ministries, e.g. Billy Graham, Stanley Jones, Will Sangster, Jack Winslow and Lee Abbey. Then prayer for the nation and people; for the Commonwealth, and for emergent nations and their training. Then for all nations, and their relationships with each other. And then finally for their own circuit and the great city of Newcastle where they live. All this praying is regular, consistent, and often very detailed, with some special concern emerging.

A few years ago, when living away from Tyneside, in one of these early morning periods they became aware that they had been leaving out one member of the family whose life had moved away from theirs. This omission was rectified. Then, says Tom, there came a day when "I was prompted to pray for him with unwonted urgency. The very words in which I prayed are written on my memory. I had special cause to remember them. I cried (after the usual mention of his name) 'O Lord, do bring him back to us, even if it be by some remarkable providence'. That prayer," says Tom, "was *precisely* answered".

Shortly afterwards he had to report a bodily irregularity to his doctor, who sent him on to the local Cottage Hospital for examination by the visiting surgeon. For eight or nine days and nights thereafter Tom knew agonising pain, and does not know whether he slept or not during that period.

Counsel was taken with a retired lady doctor of wide experience. While she was considering who might be the best specialist to consult, and the family stood waiting round Tom's bed for her telephone reply, a letter arrived "out of the blue" from the relative already mentioned. He had just landed by Comet from South Africa after a business trip and had heard of Tom's illness. He wrote offering to make arrangements for him to enter immediately the clinic of the most eminent man in this particular field. When she heard of this suggestion, the advising doctor friend was overjoyed and set aside all other names, saying, "He is tops of the world".

From the tiny Cotswold village where they were living, Tom was taken to London by Daimler Motor Ambulance. En route they had to turn aside and wait for the passing of paroxysms of pain. In the surgeon's capable hands, this pain was relieved. Tom says that he now quietly waited for the operation. It was a double major operation, brilliantly performed by two surgeons of the clinic staff. For about three weeks thereafter night and day he needed skilled nursing, but he steadily recovered without any setback.

There is no doubt that if this introduction to the specialist had not occurred, Tom would have died four years ago. The local doctor, so he learned from the family, gave him six weeks or six months to live. His wife's comment was this: "Your prayer for Cousin J. . . . has indeed been answered 'by a remarkable providence', but you never thought you'd have to go through all this." Two notes Tom adds to this account: (1) He had a telephone beside his bed and over it he heard the exchange operator of the clinic say that this cousin had enquired about his progress every morning. It was he who actually was his first visitor. (2) The lady Secretary of the clinic came in one morning and said, "Mr. Dring, your operation will cost you nothing; it is Mr. M's custom not to charge the Church anything." The material costs of the clinic were all that had to be paid.

So Tom and Florence Dring are back to their full life . . . and to their six o'clock intercession together. The experience of these two illustrates, to an extraordinary extent, the points we have been making in this chapter on "praying for others". The secrets of Forbes Robinson's remarkable influence, said those who knew him best, was due to his intercessory praying. He was always counselling others to pray in this fashion: such praying starts because of love: it is the way by which love grows, and by which one's sympathy and understanding grows, too. From the human side, there is nothing so powerful to break down barriers erected in the hearts of people to the incoming of the love of Christ. General Gordon found this, too, and so did Pastor Niemöller. During that terrible time of imprisonment and solitary confinement, the latter knew the value of other people's prayers for him; and he himself came to find the power by which he could pray—and really mean it—for his enemies and captors.

Prayer for others—though no one would dream of engaging in it for this reason—has a wonderful reflex action on the person praying. Here is what Tom says that he and his wife have discovered as a result of this intercessory praying which has meant so much to them (and to the others!) over this long period. This "great discovery", he says, was strangely unexpected: "After our initial 'Prayer of Communion' we forget ourselves in our prayers for others. And after about an hour of quiet and intercession, we find ourselves more braced for the day that lies ahead by the strength that comes to us, than by anything we have found in any other means of grace."

It would be a wonderful thing, especially, if many people, withdrawn from the field of active life by circumstance or illness, could begin to see the possibilities of intercessory prayer. They have such an opportunity to engage in it; and would find it rewarding, from every point of view. All of us, however, whoever we are, can find in this a vocation.

16. BILLY GRAHAM

PRAYER AND MASS EVANGELISM

Grant unto thy servants, that with all boldness they may speak thy word.

ACTS 4: 29

THERE CAN be no doubt that Billy Graham is the greatest exponent of mass evangelism seen in this generation. When one thinks of the figures involved in the mammoth campaigns in London, Glasgow, and still more in the cities of America, so far as figures are involved, one can delete the reference to "our generation". The number of those who have attended his meetings must now be astronomical, and the number of those registering decision also most impressive.

In Britain, Dr. Billy Graham became known through his campaign in the Spring of 1953 when, greatly daring, the Evangelical Alliance booked the Harringay Arena, seating 11,000, for a series of meetings in his name. When he came to this country, the amount of backing that he received was very small. The acknowledged Church leaders were sceptical of his success. It was thought impossible that anything like the requisite number of people could be induced, even for a night or two, to journey out to Harringay. In any case, said the pundits, the day of mass evangelism was over. The Press were frankly contemptuous, before Graham's coming, and not a little amused. Before long, Graham had won over the mass of reporters in what can only be regarded as an amazing personal triumph; and the Arena was being crowded night after night, the original period being lengthened to three months. By the time the campaign was over, Graham had the support of Bishops and Church leaders; and—by far the most important matter—thousands of people had passed through the enquiry rooms. All London, and indeed the whole country, had been forced to think, and talk, about religion once again.

Cliff College, on whose staff I was working in 1953 was one of the first institutions that openly and enthusiastically identified itself with the campaign as soon as it was planned. Prayers were made continually on its behalf. The Principal allowed his name to appear on the list of sponsors. I shall never forget the night when he and I were taken round to the room at the back of the arena on the occasion that a bus-load of our students had travelled down to Harringay. What struck me as we talked to Billy Graham was his charm and his apparent sincerity. There was no "side" about him. And what impressed me most of all was his answer to a question about the success of the mission. "It's all due," he said, "on the human side, to the volume of prayer. Why, do you know," he went on, "that Christians in Korea are actually praying for this campaign? There is a world-wide prayer concern behind it."

Later in the year, together with members of his team, he came out to the College on a day never to be forgotten. It was Whit-Monday, always celebrated as the College's Anniversary. Normally something like 10,000 people journey out into the heart of Derbyshire for that occasion. This year the number was much more like 60,000. The trouble was that the rain came, too. It started on the Sunday morning, after a week of cloudless sunshine, during which the students had prepared for this gigantic open-air meeting of unknown dimensions. In spite of the rain, the people began arriving. They stood, many of them, stolidly there, on the slopes of the hill where the platform had been erected, for hours. Billy Graham was to speak at the afternoon and evening meeting. These two were brought nearer to each other than had originally been planned. One of the astonishing things was that both times Graham began to speak, the rain stopped, and, in the afternoon, for a few minutes, the sun actually peeped out. Those who saw that solid block of people filling the hillside, waiting so patiently and good-humouredly, and who, later, saw thousands of them raising their handkerchiefs in response to the appeal at the end of the meeting, making this a sign of dedication in one of the only ways possible amidst such a vast assembly, will never forget it. For weeks after at the College we were dealing with hundreds of letters sent in by people who got into touch with us about their decision, some of these letters were from whole families.

Between the meetings we were in touch with the same unassuming young American who found time, by the way, to visit one or two of the College's invalids and shut-aways, and to pray with them. Again the same note was struck in the conversations: the secret?—the overwhelming prayer support from all over the world.

Billy Graham had been in this country before. He was then an Evangelist working with the "Youth for Christ" movement. At that time, he was effective, but nothing more. No one would have predicted the half of what was yet to happen.

The campaign at Los Angeles in 1949, so those who know his story assert, was the turning point. Three weeks had originally been allotted for the meetings at which this young Baptist minister was the main evangelist. After team meetings and inner group meetings for prayer, the conviction grew that they should go on for at least another week. It seemed strange guidance and their decision a very daring one when the weather changed and became really cold. The people, however, continued to come. Attendances, indeed, were going up. Instead of staying for a fourth week, they finally continued for eight, and the seating in the Tent was increased from 6,000 to 10,000. In the end, something like 3,000 recorded a decision for Christ. C. T. Cook, in reporting this, rightly comments that nothing like this had happened before. The popular imagination was caught, and the Press really stirred, by all that was happening, particularly when many famous stars from Hollywood were obviously impressed, and one or two converted.

At the end of this campaign Graham made the same kind of statement that I heard him make later. As first on the list of the things to which he attributed success he put "the prayers of God's people". Coupled with this was "the power of the Holy Spirit" and "the power of God's word".

This is what he said: "What power there is in prayer! I never realised it before in all my young life and ministry. It has given me a tremendous blessing in my own heart. How would you feel if you started preaching in a campaign which had had *regular* prayer meetings on its behalf for a full nine months before it started? How would you feel if every day at noon a prayer meeting was held by scores of people? How would you feel if several all-day prayer meetings had been conducted? How would you react if all-night prayer meetings had been held only a few hundred feet from the place where you were to preach the Word of God? And how would you feel if you received letters, wires and cablegrams from all parts of the world indicating that the senders were praying for you? . . . *It was the people who prayed who made the difference.*"

In this way the giant campaigns found their full impetus.

After the Harringay Campaign of 1953 in this country came the Glasgow meetings, part of the "All-Scotland Crusade", planned to take place at the Kelvin Hall in 1954. My friend, the Rev. Dr. A. Skevington Wood, then Superintendent of the Paisley Central Hall, was on the organising committee in Glasgow. Among the many interesting things which he told me about the campaign nothing impressed me more than the record of three problems which were resolved before the campaign started. Prayer was behind the solution in each case.

At the daily prayer meeting, it was the custom to pray over every item of business from the agenda of the Executive Committee. One matter concerned the location of the Crusade offices. It was obviously desirable to find a centrally-situated Headquarters. When enquiries began to be made, there were many broad smiles. Influential firms had been looking for such accommodation at the heart of Glasgow's overcrowded business area for years, and they wanted it not on a temporary, but a permanent, basis. The organising committee knew it as a direct answer to prayer when one of Scotland's leading commercial concerns offered the Crusade a complete second-floor suite of offices in Sauchiehall Street itself. Subsequently the fourth floor of the same building fell vacant and was offered just in time to house the Follow-up department before the Kelvin Hall meetings actually began.

A not-unimportant part of the preparation for these great missions concerns advertising. At a busy spot in the centre of Glasgow a vacant space, left after a large department store had been burned down, seemed "just made for the showing of an outsize sign". The ground, however, was now in the hands of the Corporation, who had already prohibited advertising there. It was assumed by many that a request for its use from the committee would be but a waste of time. Once again, after "all-prevailing prayer", an unexpected answer was given. As Glasgow residents will remember, the result was that some weeks before the Crusade began, one of the largest signs ever seen in Scotland was set up on that site to announce the coming of Billy Graham.

The third item concerned the seating at the Kelvin Hall, which in itself is nothing more than a covered exhibition centre. A special arena seating 13,000 people had to be constructed. But where was the seating to come from? A tremendous number of seats were needed for a comparatively short period. It would obviously not be right to purchase them. Once more, says Dr. Wood, "fervent effectual prayer paved the way. The Parks Superintendent of Glasgow rang up the office to ask if he could help. He had at his disposal many thousands of chairs which were not due to go into the parks until May 1st. The Crusade, he knew, finished before the end of April. He would be only too glad to offer them entirely free of cost. He not only gave them but had them freshly painted as well. Such strictly practical wonders," comments Dr. Wood, "prayer can perform!"

In this chapter we are stressing the importance of prayer in connection with mass evangelism. Everything to do with the Billy Graham campaigns underlines this. In the work of preparation, in every item of planning, in reinforcing the leader and the team, in baptising every meeting with power, in seeking to shepherd and guide all the work with individuals and with the "follow-up", prayer plays a major part.

It has always been so in all effective large-scale evangelism. D. L. Moody once said, "It is not preaching we want, it is prayer. I would rather be able to pray like Daniel than to preach like Gabriel. We do not want any more preachers in this country: we have enough. What we want is to pray. Let us open communication with heaven, and the blessing will come down." He knew the power of prayer for himself. He wanted to see a nation stirred because of the concern of praying people. He knew that prayer had an importance second to none in mass evangelism.

Lionel Fletcher held the same view. Prayer, said he, is the all-important background to evangelism. "After long years in the Christian life and in the ministry, both as a minister of churches and as an evangelist travelling the world, I am more convinced than ever that prayer is the greatest weapon we possess."

"God," said John Wesley once, "does nothing but in answer to prayer." He found it so in the days of the Evangelical Revival. In some equally famous words, he once boasted that with a hundred consecrated praying men he could turn the world upside down. You will notice, again, that the point being stressed is not the power of preaching, but of praying.

In the chapter on Edwin Orr we have already noticed that prayer was instrumental in the *Second Evangelical Awakening.* This began in America in 1857, after a group of business men had decided, spontaneously, to meet for prayer every day at noon in the vestry of the Fulton Street chapel in New York. The remarkable thing about this revival, as it spread throughout the whole of the English-speaking world, is that it was characterised by this concern for prayer. People came together to pray: in America, Ireland, Scotland, England, Wales, Australia, South Africa, New Zealand. In that time of revival it was not a matter of some one or two specially gifted evangelists being raised up—though such men did emerge, as for instance, D. L. Moody in America, and General William Booth in this country—but in the main, as Edwin Orr makes clear in his two books describing what happened, it was the work of the ordinary preacher and pastor that was revived. The power was known in every responsive, praying church.

Where do you place the emphasis for the success of evangelism? It is not only Billy Graham who replies "in persistent, faithful, fervent prayer". Every evangelist greatly used by God says the same thing; and every time of revival echoes the same message. God answers the prayers of His people. "Give me a hundred consecrated praying men and I can turn the world upside down."

17. ALEXIS CARREL

The Curative Power Of Prayer

*Heal me, O Lord, and I shall be healed; save me, and I shall
be saved, for Thou art my praise.*

JEREMIAH 17: 14

IN CHAPTER 1 we quoted the words of Hugh Redwood's
doctor after his healing in 1957: "For the first time in my life
I have witnessed, in this healing, a Divine miracle." Hugh
Redwood goes on to comment, "No doctor uses the word
'healing' lightly, especially in such a connection." Doubtless,
he was thinking of the going forward to full cure of the remarkable assuaging of his dangerous cancerous condition. But I
would take his words, also, to cover the fact that doctors, by
their training and background, are most sceptical of anything
which might be referred to as spiritual healing. Bodily conditions are susceptible to the knife and to certain medicines
—that is how a doctor is trained to think and work. Latterly,
through the development of psycho-somatic medicine, and the
increased understanding of the interaction between mind and
body, the door has opened a little wider to the curative possibilities that there are in prayer.

It is therefore of the greatest value when a medical man of
the highest order—a Nobel prize-winner—sets out his testimony to its curative effects. This Dr. Alexis Carrel has done
in a little book first published in 1947, and entitled simply,
Prayer. It was the result of the re-writing of an article that
first appeared in the *Reader's Digest*.

In his "Preface" Carrel says that this "is a very brief summing up of innumerable observations gathered during the course of a long career amongst the most diverse people. Westerners and Easterners, the sick and the healthy, Catholic priests, monks and nuns of all orders, Protestant ministers of all denominations, Rabbis, doctors and nurses, men and women of all professions and of every class of society. Besides, the author's experience as a surgeon, as a doctor, as a physiologist, the studies in the laboratory to which he devoted himself for many years, on the regeneration of the tissues and the healing of wounds, have enabled him to appreciate at their true value certain curative effects of prayer". For thirty-three years Dr. Carrel conducted biological research at the Rockefeller Institute. His Nobel prize was for work in connection with suturing blood-vessels. He also was awarded the Nordhoff-Jung medal for cancer research.

Prayer, says this great doctor, is "reaching out towards God". It is conversation between Father and child. Therefore our wants and our needs are bound to form part of it. But the loftiest part of it concerns the seeking of God's will, and the sharing of communion with Him. It is he who tells us, in this little book, the story of the peasant sitting solitary in the back pew of a church. "What are you waiting for?" asked someone coming upon him there. "I'm looking at Him and He is looking at me," was the answer.

Dr. Carrel is one who is not afraid to say that true prayer is never without result. The extent of its action on the spirit is related, he considers, to its "quality, intensity, and frequency". As a physiologist he finds himself using the analogy of the effect of an internal secretion gland, like the thyroid or the supra-renal, upon the health and tone of the body, to illustrate the effect of habitual, fervent prayer. These glands, as someone has described it, "stoke up the fires of life". By the kind of praying we are considering, says Carrel, "a flame is kindled in the depths of consciousness", which has all manner of effects in toning up the life of the one who is engaging in it. "A doctor who sees a patient giving himself to prayer," he comments, "can indeed rejoice." There speaks the voice of experience. Why? Because such a patient has access to reserves of courage and endurance, to peace and calm which in themselves, he says, are aids to healing.

In cases where medical skill is doing its best at the same time as prayer is going forward, it is difficult to assess the precise results of one or the other. Why should one try? For the medical skill, we believe, is itself an agency interpreting God's laws and using His gifts. It is not representative of *another* realm apart from that of prayer. It is all part of the same realm. And when God answers prayer it can often be through the channels of increased medical skill, through the guided intuition or understanding of a doctor or nurse.

Therefore the kind of case which provides *indisputable* evidence of the power of prayer must be outside the normal altogether. When medicine, in its present state of knowledge, has pronounced a certain condition incurable, and yet, through prayer, a cure is effected, then here, surely, we have the kind of evidence we need: or when the cure is accelerated in such a way that whereas the normal processes would carry forward over weeks or months, the healing happens almost instantaneously.

Dr. Carrel is able to speak of evidence of this kind. For a while he was on the board of examining physicians at Lourdes. This is a Roman Catholic shrine where many people have been brought to a condition of deep faith and fervent prayer. We believe that there is no magic in the place, as such, but there *is* effectiveness in the attitude to which it has, especially in past days, brought many people. Over the years, Dr. Carrel states quite categorically, and especially forty or fifty years ago—before the place lost its atmosphere of quiet and contemplation and became a garish tourist centre—indisputable cures of the kind we have in mind have occurred.

In his testimony he states, "patients have been cured almost instantaneously of affections such as lupus of the face, cancer, kidney troubles, ulcers, tuberculosis of the lungs, of the bones or peritoneum. . . .The miracle is characterised by extreme acceleration of the normal processes of healing. Never has such an acceleration been observed up till now in the course of their experiences by surgeons and physiologists."

There are two other most valuable things to note from Dr. Carrel's account of his own observations. In the swift "miracle", the order of events is almost always this: first a feeling of great pain and acute awareness of the malady—almost, one would imagine, as if the point of disease were being grasped by a mighty hand—"It is here you ail"—and then, as swiftly and certainly, comes the feeling of peace and wholeness. "In a few seconds, at most a few hours, the symptoms disappear and the anatomic lesions mend."

The second thing he notes is that it is not a necessary condition of these happenings that the patient should be praying, or even that he or she should be a believer! Other people's prayer can act as the agent. "Little children still unable to speak and unbelievers have been cured, but near them, some one prayed."

The story is told that Dr. Carrel's wife was a member of the nursing staff at Lourdes, and that one day she was holding up a woman, dying of cancer, in order that she might be able to breathe. The dying woman in her arms was, however, healed! And this not because she was praying for herself, but for the reverse reason. The sight of somebody else's suffering, at that moment, had so moved the poor woman, that she prayed most fervently, even though it might have been with her dying breath, for the other. And while she prayed, she was cured. We referred to the reflex influence of our prayers, in our chapter on "Praying for Others". Let us notice here and now against what background Alexis Carrel could write, "Prayer made for another is always more fruitful than when made for oneself."

"Such," says this doctor and physiologist, "are the results of prayer of which I have a sure knowledge." Isn't that testimony of the utmost value?

In 1935, Dr. Carrel published a much larger volume which endeavours to collate within its covers much of our modern understanding of *Man the Unknown*. Here are details concerning our physical frame, our glandular system, our chemical components, our mental structure. The same unhesitating testimony is given about the curative power of prayer. He also makes the same point as Steinmetz made, in the words quoted in our Introduction. The miraculous healings recorded by the Medical Bureau of Lourdes, he contends, establish beyond any doubt the connection between prayer and curative power. "Such facts," he states, "are of profound significance. They show the reality of certain relations, of still unknown nature, between psychological and organic processes. They prove the objective importance of the spiritual activities, which hygienists, physicians, educators, and sociologists have almost always neglected to study. They open to man a new world."

What we have done in this chapter is to isolate the testimony of a man who had every right to know what he was talking about. We are not saying, nor did he say, that prayer for healing is always answered in terms of the actual request made. He says that prayer depends—from our side of reality—on such factors as its quality, intensity, and frequency. Jesus, you will remember, had much to say about faith and about persistency in prayer! Alexis Carrel says, too, that unselfish prayer —prayer for others—is far more potent, even for ourselves, than prayer selfishly made and selfishly directed. The important thing, however, is this, that this gifted and qualified medical man sets it on record, as the result of long experience and close observation, that prayer has curative power.

18. LESLIE D. WEATHERHEAD

PRAYER FOR HEALING

I will pray with the spirit, and I will pray with the understanding also.

I CORINTHIANS 14: 15

IN THE crowded church, as the hour of seven o'clock approaches, one can see the congregation leaning forward, ready to enter into the "Fellowship of Silence". It is true that among the fourteen hundred people present there are many visitors, for this church is one to which visitors to London, both from the provinces and from far overseas, make their way. But they can easily follow, and join in the customary procedure. Others in the congregation could be called "occasional" visitors, coming in from the outer suburbs once in a while: but they, like the regular members, having been before, know what to expect.

On the whole, then, it is a trained congregation that now follows the minister as he guides them into this act of imaginative intercession. Many of them, too, know of cases that have been helped by the remembrance in the "Fellowship of Silence". So that the spirit of faith is abroad as the quietness deepens and together the worshippers seek a special sense of the presence of God.

The vibrant, persuasive voice of the preacher, which possesses a hint both of laughter and tenderness, is sounding: "Together we are about to link the thought of someone in need with the power of Christ. First of all, our prayers are asked for a Nurse who herself has fallen ill. Nineteen years of age, and a member of this Church, she is suffering from so-and-so. For some days she has not been able to sleep without drugs, nor to take food. Her temperature is very high. . . . Realise that Christ is with her now. In imagination stand with Him by her bedside; and believe that He is touching her life with power, healing her—now."

There is silence for a moment. Then the voice continues, "Hold your mind steadily there, concentrating on Christ's power, His knowledge, and His love. Let your prayer do what your arms would have done in the days of Christ. Lift her into His presence, in imagination; and *see* her becoming well, as His healing power is being made manifest in her body now."

Again there is silence. Then another case is mentioned: this time a boy, whose Christian name is given, and for whose need the love and sympathy of the congregation is aroused as the chronic nature of his illness is outlined in a few, deft words.

"Please, as you pray, don't feel sorry for him. If you do, instead of helping him, you'll be helping to confirm the trouble in him. Rather, see him getting well. Christ is with him. Concentrate on that."

Perhaps another case is brought before the congregation, no more. This time no name is given, for the trouble is a mental one, and the name has been withheld; but enough is said to help the congregation to direct their prayers towards the person concerned.

It may well be that as we leave the building, though we have listened to fine preaching and shared in communal worship at a high level, the memory that most fills our minds is of those moments when so vividly we felt the presence of Christ and knew His power was flowing to aid people. As we thought of that poor, demented woman it was as if we *saw* Him speaking to her, calming the storm within, and saw the look of peace that lit up her face. To come away like that has often been the experience of worshippers in the City Temple congregation.

One would be hard put to it to label this church and congregation effectively. It is, technically, a Congregational church, whose home in Holborn is just within the boundaries of the City of London. Former ministers have been Joseph Parker, R. J. Campbell, F. W. Norwood. Its present leader is an ordained Methodist minister, who within recent years, while serving in this Congregational church, was elected President of the Methodist Conference! And the church, bombed out of its original building in the Second World War, met first in an Anglican church, and then, after several other places, including the Friends Meeting House at Euston, settled for many years prior to its own rebuilding in a Presbyterian church, and all this by invitation of the churches concerned.

Dr. Leslie Weatherhead, the minister, was born in London, but grew up in Leicester, where his parents were members of the Saxby Road Methodist Church. He was trained at Richmond College; went into circuit at Aldershot; and was then transferred to the English church in Madras. From thence, in the First World War, he entered the Indian Army, serving as Lieutenant and then Captain. Before the war ended, he had been transferred to chaplaincy work. His first church, on his return home, was the Oxford Road chapel in Manchester, and from there he went to Brunswick Chapel, Leeds, where his phenomenally "popular" ministry really began. By this time his initial interest in psychology had developed into a passionate concern to link its findings with the truths of religion. He began an extensive psychiatric practice himself, and won the co-operation of many doctors and psychologists in the work that he was doing. When finally he came to London to the City Temple, his fame in this field was widespread. Among many books that he has written are a number on psychological subjects, culminating in his large-scale work on *Psychology, Religion and Healing*, for which the University of London awarded him a doctorate.

It was over a period of eleven years at Leeds, and now for more than twice that period at the City Temple, that he has continued this practice of intercession for individually named sick people in his evening service. As he so rightly claims, these thirty years and more of experience give him some authority to speak on the subject.

He thinks that prayer is a means of co-operating with God in a patient's recovery, and that, medical, surgical and nursing skills are, similarly, ways of co-operating with God. These, however, are usually matters entirely on the physical level. Prayer is co-operation on the mental and spiritual plane. Prayer is not to be thought of as a method of automatic magic in the least comparable to the working of "a penny in the slot". Nor does it displace medical skill. Always it can support it. Sometimes it can do things not available to medical science because of the kind of power it brings into operation on the spiritual level. "In every case of illness and suffering," says L. D. Weatherhead, "we must find the relevant way of co-operating with God." No one, he says, would think of praying about his teeth: he would go to the dentist! A thorn is to be pulled out, not prayed about!

A favourite quotation of Dr. Weatherhead's is from Sir Oliver Lodge's book, *Man and the Universe*, in which the scientist writes, "Even in medicine, for instance, it is not really absurd to suggest that drugs and no prayer may be almost as foolish as prayer and no drugs." It is quite evident that Leslie Weatherhead gives prayer a high place as a therapeutic agent, and at the same time he does not regard the use of faith and prayer as a substitute for medical skill and attention.

What then of the results of the kind of praying that has gone on in the "Fellowship of Silence"? "I will only say," he writes in an article in the *Methodist Recorder* dated 3rd February

1949, "that when one has collected, as I have, a large number of cases of patients, given up by doctors, who have recovered after prayer: when one has noted that a significant proportion has taken a turn for the better during the time prayer was offered, one can confidently say that, if any drug were discovered about which the same could be said, it would be universally used and acclaimed as the curative agent, even though, like prayer, it frequently disappointed those who resorted to it."

It was in the pages of the *Methodist Recorder* for January 1949 that the case of David Hughes was reported. David's mother, before her marriage, had been a member of Brunswick Chapel, and doubtless, while there, had joined many times in the "Fellowship of Silence" for other people. Now, on January 25th, 1948, from the little Welsh village where she now lived, she sent a wire to Dr. Weatherhead, couched in terms of desperation. David, aged four-and-a-half, was seriously ill with nephritis (inflammation of the kidneys). The congregation began to pray for him, and did so every Sunday evening thereafter until the middle of March. An immense volume of interest was created for the lad.

Depressing reports continued. On February 11th, Mrs. Hughes wrote, "All the doctors agree that permanent damage has been done to the kidneys and that David will never be the same again." He was sent home from hospital, plainly because nothing more could be done for him. On February 19th, the mother's message read, "He is still with us, but desperately ill. The poor little chap can keep nothing down and we expect the end at any moment. The doctor says he will get sleepier and sleepier, until he sinks into a coma and then dies." She added, "I wrote a letter to you on Monday saying that by the time you received it he would be dead. But I did not post it and tried to keep up my faith."

Then, on February 24th, there came this: "A very hurried note to tell you the wonderful news that David has taken a turn for the better. A week ago there was absolutely no hope, but on Friday his kidneys began working again and the swelling began to decrease. . . . It is nothing less than a miracle and we are all convinced it is in reponse to prayer. The wonderful and amazing part is that since his life was given up, no drugs were given and the doctor who told me last Thursday that he would pass into a coma cannot understand it at all. He says, 'If David can recover without drugs, it seems useless to give him any more.'"

On March 5th, the boy said to his mother, as she showed him the service papers from the City Temple, and he saw his own name in print, "Mummy, write and tell that Minister of the big London Church, that I am better."—And so he was! Further examinations proved that no damage had been done to the kidneys at all! Six months after the appeal for help, David was reported to be running about, a normal child again. One of the doctors—who had declared the case hopeless—said to his father, "Well, all I can say is that prayer has succeeded where medicine failed." "I have attended a number of similar cases and never saw one recover," the specialist wrote to Dr. Weatherhead. "I had to tell the father that there was definitely no hope whatever . . . . Within about a week after this David's condition changed for the better and in a very short time he was practically normal, which was most extraordinary to me."

I have another cutting from an earlier *Methodist Recorder*, dated Jan. 6th 1938. In this Leslie Weatherhead tells of a girl of seventeen, who five months before had come to him at the City Temple for psychological help. He arranged for her to see a Harley Street specialist, who over some years has given help at the City Temple psychiatric clinic. After six separate hours spent with the patient, he felt beaten, and sadly sent her home with the message that nothing could be done for her.

After some days of uneasiness at the thought of their lack of ability to help, Dr. Weatherhead tells how one night he dreamt of this girl, and on waking put her name down on the pad by his bedside. The next day he wrote to her mother that on the following Sunday they would pray for her. On that day, the congregation were asked to do so. This time no names were mentioned, nor was the nature of the illness revealed in any detail. Yet from that night, the illness vanished, and the girl was perfectly well.

Dr. Weatherhead asked the psychiatrist whether he had possibly started a process in his interviews which could have resulted in the cure. Very quietly he said, "No. I did nothing. It is to me a miracle, an act of God Himself without any help from us except our praying."

Twelve years afterwards, in 1951, Weatherhead mentioned this incident, together with others where help had been given through the City Temple intercession, in *Psychology*, *Religion and Healing*, and added this note, "Enquiry shows that this cure has been maintained up to the time of writing these words—more than twelve years after the patient was first seen."

There is an incident which Dr. Weatherhead has described to his congregation at least twice, so deep an impression did it make on him, and so important a message does it carry. It happened at Brunswick, Leeds. A girl was converted at one of his services. Six weeks later she came into his vestry after the evening service and said, "It's no good. I'm giving up Christianity. It doesn't work." She had a bad temper, and, in spite of prayers and attempts to master it, it had not gone. Nothing that Weatherhead said seemed to make any difference. The next person to enter the vestry told of a daughter who had been converted, whose changed life had affected the whole atmosphere of the home. "It's because of her I'm here tonight." It was this girl's father! "Go after her," exclaimed the minister. "She's just been in here. Bring her back; and say what you've just said to me in front of her." Sometimes we think that nothing is happening as a result of our praying, but we are wrong, especially if the subject happens to be ourselves. We are standing too near to that subject to be able to judge properly! Nor can we always tell how our prayer for another is affecting them. But no real prayer is wasted. If it really is an attempt to co-operate with God, He takes it and uses it, even if in a way different from the way in which we wished Him first to answer it.

"When we pray for a person," Dr. Weatherhead once said to his congregation, "there goes from our hearts to God an expression of love and care and faith which, like the oxygen tent over the bed of a lung patient is a physical treatment . . . provides the kind of spiritual atmosphere in which God can more potently do His will, which is to cure the sufferer. I can only tell you dogmatically that, again and again, a patient has taken a turn for the better at the very moment when a thousand people in a City Temple service have been offering prayer for his recovery."

This provides us with a most important testimony, and a great encouragement to pray for sick friends—to do this individually and to learn how to do it, imaginatively and positively, as the City Temple congregation does in its "Fellowship of Silence".

One of the concerns which the minister of the City Temple obviously has is that the imagination of each individual member of the congregation should be strongly roused. He wants each person to *see* the patient and to *see* Jesus. By this "imaginative sympathy" a bridge is made between the worshippers and the person in need, who, by the way, knows that he is being remembered. The strong thought at the very same time, of Christ and of His power to aid, reinforced as for example by such words as "Do for her in your prayer what your arms would have done for her in Galilee. Carry her into His presence," is vital praying, linking sufferer and Healer. It is intercession of a deep order.

Another element to note is that of the constructive, upbuilding use of the imagination that is involved. One is not encouraged to see the sufferer *under* the trouble, but triumphing over it by the grace of Christ. "Negative thoughts" about the sufferer and his complaint are, indeed, discouraged. The "sympathy" that is being asked for is not a negative state of being sorry for the person. It is encouraged only that everyone may have a vital appreciation of the patient's need.

The supreme insistence of the one guiding this period of imaginative intercession is, however, not upon the patient or his need, but upon Christ and His power to heal and aid. If only patient and congregation alike could *know* this what might not be possible! His power to aid, His knowledge of our needs and His capacity to answer them, is as strong as ever.

THE FINAL SECRET

19. OSWALD CHAMBERS

God Himself is the Answer

Fear not, Abram, I am thy shield, and thy exceeding great reward.

GENESIS 15: 1

THE FACT that we know of Oswald Chambers at all is in itself remarkable. He died in November 1917, at the age of forty-three, while serving as a Chaplain with the Y.M.C.A. in Egypt. Only a comparative handful of people knew him by that time. After his death, his widow and a group of friends began to issue in his name a series of books and pamphlets which have circulated now throughout the world. Thousands of copies have been sold, and "Oswald Chambers" has, in this way, helped untold numbers of people. Of him it is literally true that "he being dead yet speaketh".

All this has been made possible because his wife took full shorthand notes of his lectures, sermons and addresses. Oswald Chambers believed implicitly in God's government of the haphazard. A life placed in His hands could be used in ways full of wonder and surprise. "Let God engineer," was one of his favourite phrases. His forty-three years are a set of variations on this theme, but nothing illustrates it more than what has occurred after what must have seemed his untoward death. By this his words have now been released to reach folk everywhere.

It was as an Art student that he began. Scholarships took him to Edinburgh, where he became a University prizeman in Fine Art and Archaeology. One night while sitting alone at Arthur's Seat it was as if he heard a voice saying to him, "I want you in My service—but I can do without you". Returning to his lodgings he found, as if by chance, that someone had sent him a report of a Bible Training College at Dunoon. To this rather unusual College (there were no stated fees: men gave what they could) O.C. went. He was to teach Fine Arts and to study theological subjects. In 1898 (he was then twenty-four) he became a tutor, teaching not only his own subject but Logic, Moral Philosophy and Psychology, subjects which he had largely prepared in private study.

Though his life passed through several phases ("Consistency is the hobgoblin of little minds" was another of his sayings), from the first O.C. was an explorer in spiritual matters and an adventurer in prayer. A niece, who remembers him as a constant visitor to her home during the Dunoon period, recalls that he was a very early riser. He could be found at six o'clock in the morning, wrapped in his plaid for warmth, with teapot near at hand, reading, writing, or on his knees in prayer. "The naturalness of his religion impressed us children," she said years afterwards. "Looking back, I realise that he came into our quiet home life with its parochial outlook like a west wind, waking us up and bringing an exciting sense of limitless possibilities."

Later, Chambers started a Bible Training College himself in a house on the North side of Clapham Common. It had a similar aim and background to the Dunoon Training College. A student has given us an impression of her first days there. Looking round the dining table she thought that never had a quainter collection of people gathered together in a training school—men and women of all ages and occupations and social groups. From where he sat at the head of the long table O.C.'s eye met hers, and she heard him say, with a twinkle, "You won't need Punch here."

It was in May 1915 that he offered his services as a chaplain and went out to Egypt under the auspices of the Y.M.C.A. It was typical of him that no arrangements had been made about salary, and also typical of his story that his wife and daughter arrived in Egypt to join him only a day or two before a ban was placed on the arrival of any more women in the country.

The way O.C. did his chaplaincy work was thoroughgoing. All the time his eye was on ultimate things. No one was in any doubt about the purpose for which he was amongst them. And how he impressed some of the Gallipoli men! "This keen-faced, lean, alert man was the greatest man I have ever met," said one Australian soldier. "Here, one felt, was a prophet, a teacher, a disciple of Jesus Christ."

It was in the evenings that he held the meetings and gave the talks, notes of which were taken down by Mrs. Chambers. Brown-faced soldiers, in shorts and open-necked shirts, would begin to drift into the hut, maybe looking at the row of books set out at the back, or staring, some of them quite uncomprehendingly, at the blackboard on which O.C. had already chalked an outline of his lecture, or drawn some illustrative diagram. Then, just before O.C. himself, the ladies of the Y.M.C.A. staff would enter. A hymn and a prayer, and then the Bible Study, for which, said Chambers, men would come. What they wanted, he declared, was "instruction in Christian matters, much more than the old form of evangelistic services". And instruction—often on the deepest level—they received.

Here for example is how he began a talk in that hut in Zeitoun on the subject "What's the good of prayers?"—"It is only when a man flounders beyond any grip of himself and cannot understand things that he really prays. It is not part of the natural life of a man to pray. By 'natural' I mean the ordinary, sensible, healthy, worldly-minded life. We hear it said that a man will suffer in his life if he does not pray; I question it. Prayer is an interruption to personal ambition, and no man who is busy has time to pray. What will suffer is the life of God in him, which is nourished not by food but by prayer." That would certainly jerk those soldiers into listening! This kind of teaching, they would think, isn't the usual kind of approach to this subject. As they listened further they would be quite certain about that. They would be required to give all their attention. On that evening—as on any other—their minds would be at full stretch!

Behind O.C.'s words was his own experience—that of a man who had set himself to follow only God's way. Endeavouring to do this had caused him to do many quixotic things, clean against all counsels of prudence. "Everything is possible to God," he would say, "and I'm his bairn." Only those who have ventured fully on uncharted seas, believing in the certainty of God's piloting, have any right to speak of certain reaches of faith. Chambers had done that.

In a pamphlet entitled *The Discipline of Prayer* we find him revealing something of his own methods in his "Morning Watch". As always, he insists that the whole point is to share "intimacy of relation with our Father". He tells how he has found it a valuable experience to re-write the Psalms, pouring out these same petitions and praises, but making of them now a channel of his own self-expression. At other times, though but rarely he says, he has used a horology like Bishop Andrews' Devotions. The writing out of his own desires, thoughts and petitions was a method still more useful. By doing this, O.C. came to see exactly what he really thought and wanted to say; and, having come to that knowledge, he said it, quite simply, to God.

O.C. had a way of characterising prayer as "stupid". On the ground of ordinary commonsense notions, he would say, it really is stupid. What is needed is the spirit of the childlike, simple, supernatural saint. Try to explain prayer and how it works, on the line of reason, and it is nonsense. Prayer is a

supernatural act, motivated by God and entered into at His
invitation, made possible by His Redemption. One is brought
into the life of God through Jesus. That new life in Him needs
to be maintained. "You may not need to pray," O.C. declared,
"but Jesus Christ within you does." In this way, in James
Montgomery's words, prayer is the Christian's "vital breath".
By it, the life of the Son of God within us is nourished and kept
alive.

We can see how a man with this background lifts us above
little thoughts of prayer. The substance of his teaching is that
God Himself is the answer to our prayers. You remember how
God said to Abram in Genesis 15: 1, "Fear not, Abram: I am
thy shield, and thy exceeding great reward"? Greater than the
blessings that God can bestow is this intimacy of communion
with Him who sends the blessings. O.C. came to know this,
too. In itself, the getting of things from God, he declared, is a
very elementary form of prayer. Just as in extremity men are
driven to pray, so the sense of need sometimes drives us to
pray for specific things for ourselves and others. But the
"answers" that come in that way are not the true goal. If we
remain satisfied with them we have been diverted. "Prayer is
getting into perfect communion with God."

All his life, Oswald had prayed the simple direct prayer of
asking. When five years old he set his heart on having two
guinea pigs, and he prayed nightly for them. He was certain
they would come—and in the end they did. So "original" were
his prayers as a child that his mother and some of the older
members of the family would listen sometimes on the stairs to
hear him pray. His brother wrote this of him: "this childlike
confidence in God, enlarged and enriched in wonderful ways,
was the same in essence and simplicity whether he asked for
guinea pigs or railway fares or passage money to Japan". Make
no doubt about it, O.C. never ceased "asking" in prayer. He
knew that we have our Lord's warrant for this, and during his

lifetime he knew hundreds of quite amazing "answers" concerning things about which he had prayed. But it remained true that the most wonderful thing he had discovered about prayer is that God Himself is the Answer. In that book of devotional extracts from his messages, *My Utmost for His Highest*, he says, "Whenever the insistence is on the point that God answers prayer, we are off the track. The meaning of Prayer is that we get hold of God, not of the Answer."

> Thy gifts, alone, cannot suffice
> Unless Thyself be given;
> Thy presence makes my paradise,
> And where Thou art is heaven.

If, after some passionate prayer of our own, we have been perplexed because of a failure to discern an answer, perhaps these words will help: "Our understanding of God is the answer to prayer; getting things from God is God's indulgence of us. When God stops giving us things, He brings us into the place where we can begin to understand Him. As long as we get from God everything we ask for, we never get to know Him, we look upon Him as a blessing-machine. . . . 'Your Father knoweth what things ye have need of, before ye ask Him.' Then why pray? To get to know your Father. It is not sufficient for us to say, 'Oh yes, God is love,' we have to know He is love, we have to struggle through until we do see He is love and justice. Then our prayer is answered."

Oswald Chambers could look back over his own life and experience and realise that there were times when the exact answer to his prayer, deep, passionate and real, had been denied. The answer came on an altogether deeper level: through that period of praying, through the concern so deeply shared with God, he had come to know God better. To some, this might seem to be an evasion. Scripture plainly says that God answers prayer—prayer uttered in faith, and in the name of Christ. What Chambers had come to see is that God brings us to a point in our experience when we are able to accept it, when the answer transcends altogether what we have been asking for: an experience of God, of contact with Him, comes flooding in, that makes our actual request seem altogether puny. And if it be that the request is set aside or deferred—and God's answer is sometimes "No": a definite "No" sounding in our spirit—we have had an answer that fulfils what is the deepest need for us and for others. It is this renewed and deepened contact with God that for us, at the time, is the perfect answer. And, if our prayer has been for others, at that time, too, we know that their ultimate safety and destiny is assured by the same Fatherly care and love.

Only those who, like Oswald Chambers, have known the depth of this experience and this assurance, know that this so far from being a rejection, or a refusal of our prayer, brings us to the place for which all prayer is made. We are in vital communion with Him. Our wants, our needs, our requests are known—and will be dealt with. Here and now, we are answered. His Spirit meets our own.

20. THOMAS KELLY

LIVING FROM THE CENTRE

Ye are the temple of God, and the Spirit of God dwelleth in you.
I CORINTHIANS 3: 16

IT IS always difficult to pick from within one's own generation the books, music, art, pictures, etc., that will endure.
One feels, however, that a small book that was first printed in
November 1943 under the title *A Testament of Devotion* will
last. It consists of a biographical memoir of Thomas R. Kelly,
whose addresses, five of them, on "The Light Within",
"Holy Obedience", "The Blessed Community", "The
Eternal Now and Social Concern", and "The Simplification
of Life", fill the rest of the book.

Its theme concerns the great discovery of Kelly's life: that
it is possible, as he says, to "live from the centre". This kind
of life, he declares, "is a life of unhurried peace and power.
It is simple. It is serene. It is amazing. It is triumphant. It is
radiant. It takes no time, but it occupies all our time. And it
makes our life programmes new and overcoming. We need
not get frantic. He is at the helm. And when our little day is
done we lie down quietly in peace, for all is well". Is not that
the way of life for which all are seeking? Expressed in another
way, that to which Kelly is pointing is "the life of ceaseless
prayer".

Kelly's father died when he was four, and his mother continued to work the farm and deliver butter and eggs in the

174

near-by village in order to support the family. Theirs was a Quaker home in Ohio, into which Thomas had been born in 1893. One can tell the quality of this mother of his: after another six years, in order that her children might have the further educational advantages that the town could give, she moved to Wilmington, started learning typing and book-keeping, and took over an office job there.

It was in January 1938 that Professor Thomas Kelly, as by now he had come to be, lecturer at Haverford in Philosophy, Greek and Oriental, surprised his hearers at a series of lectures by striking an altogether new note. The lectures were being given to the Friends' Meeting at Coulter Street, Germantown. The new note rang in his voice, and was detectable in what he had to say. People were deeply moved. "This is the authentic note," they said. The lecturer himself said of these lectures that "they wrote themselves". What had happened was that a man who for many years had been searching had arrived. From within his own experience he could say now to the seeker after reality, "God *can* be found. . . . There is a Divine Centre into which your life can slip, a new and absolute orientation in God, a Centre where you live with Him and out of which you see all of life, through new and radiant vision, tinged with new sorrows and pangs, new joys unspeakable and full of glory."

Kelly was forty-two years of age when he began to talk to people in this way. Years of patient service and questing were issuing in harvest. Hitherto, Kelly's search for truth had been that of a philosopher. Trained as a scientist, his career had led him into the life of the college and academy. During his student days he was fortunate to come into touch with that great Quaker teacher, Rufus Jones. Later, Prof. A. N. White-head exerted a deep influence on him. But he was the academi-cian. In this middle period of his life he declared that rigorous scholarship was the goal of his desire. "I merely want to write and work as a typical scholar," he confided to one of his friends, and to another, "I am hopelessly committed to the life of a scholar. . . . I can't be anything but this kind of person, and I might as well surrender to it."

Then there came opportunity to travel to Hawaii, and there to teach in the University. These eighteen months of transplanting, though they undermined his physical health, brought him into enlivening touch with another culture and with different ways of living. In this half-way house between East and West, he became acquainted with oriental philosophers. Returning to settle at Haverford, in the autumn of 1937, the new experience came to him, as a result of which he began to speak with assurance about "living from the centre".

"No one knows exactly what happened," says his biographer, his friend Douglas V. Steere, "but a strained period was over. He moved towards adequacy."

From as far afield as Germany, calls came for Kelly to speak to groups of people. These were not academic talks that were being asked for: the Friends were anxious to hear from him the authentic tidings he could now give concerning God's working. One of the results of his new attitude was that, wherever he now went, he found a depth of fellowship with all sorts of people. Months in Germany still further deepened the process which had been going on within him. There are many who can testify that among the Friends in Germany he left an abiding memory. After his return to America, one of the experiences of which he spoke was of an occasion when he stood in the great Cathedral of Cologne. Those were the days of 1938. It was as if for a moment, he said, God showed him something of the total suffering of humanity, allowing him a share in this divine burden. Said Kelly, without God's help even the sense of what it was was unbearable.

Around Kelly, back again at Haverford, a little group formed itself quite naturally. They read between them books on prayer and the devotional life—Brother Lawrence, Augustine's

Confessions, Père Grou, the Little Flowers of St. Francis, Laubach's *Letters of a Modern Mystic*, as well as the New Testament and the Psalms. One of the students who was a member of this group says, "Tom was always telling funny stories about the deepest thoughts." Obviously, he did not let his group become too mock-pious or introspective. It is on record, too, that this same Professor startled some of his colleagues at the same time by a new directness and simplicity in speaking about spiritual things. All was new, fresh and real. The academician had burst through into the realms of life.

He was only forty-seven when he died. It so happens that the first three chapters in *The Testament of Devotion* were all written within a few days of his sudden home call. We quote chiefly from them in order to illustrate his special contribution to our theme.

Within us all there is a "sanctuary of the soul", where communion with God is possible. As Kelly describes it in his first essay, using another of the many pictures that help us to realise what it is and how it functions, it is "a Light Within": a centre made for creative response, a place where God's light glows, where understanding comes of who God is and what He is saying to us. The heart and secret of the devotional life is to discover the Light Within, and tend this vital flame. Just as surely as Brother Lawrence did, so this modern Quaker counsels the development of "mental habits of inward orientation". And he, too, out of his own experience, tells us about the difficulties, especially during the first months, weeks and days, of reasserting this habit of continually "practising the Presence". At first, we have to swing, consciously, from immersion in the world's affairs to a deliberate remembrance of God and thought of the Inner Light; but after some time spent in building ourselves up in this recollection of God, there comes a sense of a power undergirding all our living. Then it is, as

Brother Lawrence himself declared, that the times when we are busiest about ordinary affairs are, in a measure, no different from our times of conscious and deliberate worship. The inner centre has become dominant, and the sense of God's continual presence an assured fact.

It is for our own good, Kelly discovered, that, at times, this sense of "simultaneity", in which we can be concurrently immersed in both levels (that of "outer things" and the "Inner Light"), lapses and fades. Were it not so, our spiritual pride would assert itself. Indeed, the actual cause of the fading of the experience is in all probability due to an assertion, within ourselves, that it is by our own higher spirituality that we have succeeded in developing this. As in all these matters, we need to know that God is the initiator. All is of His grace and power.

How did Kelly find means to aid the processes of continual inward prayer within himself? He formulated certain phrases, full of meaning to him personally, repeating them, and mentally falling back on them again and again. During the first weeks, he tells us, he must have gone over them countless times, not with any idea of "being heard for his much speaking", but because this method helped his consciousness of God's continual presence and blessing. Such phrases, he says, should not be stereotyped. They can be changed and varied. They should be one's own, even if they are culled from someone else, or from the scriptures. "Thine only", was a phrase that evidently meant much to Kelly at this time, and, from the Psalms, "My soul panteth after Thee, O God". If he found that he had forgotten God for quite a long period, following Brother Lawrence, he wasted no time in self-recrimination; but, like the monk before him, he discovered that the thing to do was swiftly to resume the communion that had been interrupted: "This is what happens unless you help me," he, too, could say to God.

178

The result of this habit, persisted in over a period of time, is that one passes into a state when it is no longer necessary to use verbal formulae. Swiftly and immediately, anywhere, one can lift one's heart to God, or realise His presence in that inner sanctuary at the centre. What happens, as Kelly discovered afresh, is that from that centre, "a Greater prays in us". We are being used, says Kelly, to be "prayed through". God, who is with us and in us, uses the temple of our poor life as a centre through which His love and concern is flowing into the life of the world. This is the kind of thing that St. Paul had in mind when he spoke of "the Spirit praying within us".

It is given to different branches of the Christian Church, and to different groups of Christians, to emphasise some particular aspect of Christian truth and experience. The special contribution of the Society of Friends, as Kelly himself witnesses, lies in its reminder of the fact that life is to be lived from its inner centre. Interestingly enough, earlier in this book, we have listened to a French Catholic, Paul Claudel, making the same point. It is in this centre that God comes to us, there that we hear His whisper, know His guidance. From that point we pray; from that point we draw our real life, and have communion with God.

> The outward God he findeth not,
> Who finds not God within.

"'There is a divine Abyss within us all," says Thomas Kelly, "a holy Infinite Centre, a Heart, a Life who speaks in us and through us to the world. . . . At times we have followed the Whisper, and amazing equilibrium of life, amazing effectiveness of living set in. But too many of us have heeded the Voice only at times. Only at times have we submitted to His holy guidance. We have not counted this Holy Thing within to be the most precious thing in the world. We have not surrendered *all else*, to attend to it alone." This is the way forward—to live from the Centre, to build up our life from that point where God is known, and where He speaks and prays within us. All else is worth surrendering for this. And the "all else", as Kelly knew, is given back to us in a new way when we have discovered this new way of living.

EPILOGUE

EPILOGUE

Verily, verily, I say unto thee: Except a man be born again he cannot see the kingdom of God.

JOHN 3: 3

I'T HAS been more than worth while to collect these modern examples of men and women praying. What a diverse group they make when gathered together—Quaker, Anglican, Free Church; folk outside the denominations, and folk right at their centre; men, women; leaders, missionaries, ordained ministers and laymen—and they are just as diversified in their approach to our subject!

We set out to illustrate the fact that prayer affords a living field for exploration. These folk, surely, have demonstrated that most adequately. Equally, they make clear that in this field there are many ways, many types and methods.

For ourselves, we must remember that the way for one person is not always the way for another. For each of us God has His "secret stair": His special way of approach to our soul and mind. What other people have attempted can be a spur, and the record of their adventures may yield many a suggestion that is helpful; but what becomes really valuable to us are our own discoveries: the convictions that we arrive at because our experience is behind them.

Prayer is living communion with God, often touched off, in the first instance, because of some supreme need. Faith is its first necessity. "He that cometh to God must believe that He is, and that He is a rewarder of them that diligently

183

seek Him." Prayer begins with that spirit and understanding, and goes on from that point: without this, no amount of elaborate imitation of anyone else's praying methods avails in the least. Major Lewis Hastings in his travel-book, *Dragons are Extra*, tells of a traveller in West Africa who noticed throughout an area a number of neat structures of sticks and twigs arranged on the ground. They looked like fires that were waiting to be lit. He was told that that is exactly what they were—the work of chimpanzees imitating man, but not knowing how to kindle the vital flame! How disappointed the apes must have been, time and again, when they built their pyramids of stick, and found that nothing happened. The flame was not there.

Something has been assumed throughout this book that must be stressed before it closes. The vital necessity in all *Christian* prayer is the existence of a special relationship with Jesus. These men and women pray as part of His company, as members of the Society of the Redeemed, as those who know the powers of the Kingdom.

Hugh Redwood, with whom we began, stresses this in *Practical Prayer*. He paraphrases Christ's conversation with Nicodemus in John 2: 23 ff in such a way that we, too, realise that Jesus is talking to us in turn about a *new* Kingdom and about a radical change in human nature by which we enter into it. Unless a man is born again—the astonished religious leader was told—he cannot see, nor understand, nor enter into this other realm with its higher laws, where Jesus works and operates.

Stanley Jones says that the gateway to prayer is "surrender". This may be thought of as the human side of the experience by which the "new birth" takes place. It is made possible by Christ, and supremely through what we come to know of God's Love and Forgiveness in Christ's mighty acts for us—in His coming into our world, in His Dying for us, and in His Rising Again from the dead. The Cross is the point where the greatest obstruction between God and man can be removed. We come to see that in His Death, Christ was dealing with this barrier—finding a way of victory over this thing in human nature which defeats even the best of us. By faith, we identify ourselves with what Christ did for us on Calvary, and find that the same love, mercy and power are available at this instant, *now*. The barrier can go. We find ourselves at one with God. We know our sins forgiven, and find ourselves in living contact with all the forces of the Kingdom.

Thus it is that Oswald Chambers can say, "God answers prayer on the ground of Redemption and on no other ground." "When a man is born from above, the life of the Son of God is born in him, which is nourished not by food but by prayer. . . . Prayer is the nourishing of the life of the Son of God within you."

Our very desire to foster this life within us, and to enter into our heritage in the Kingdom, henceforth living "no more unto ourselves, but unto Him", should be to discover from Him, above all others, what are the secrets of His way of life. Throughout this book, the folk whose experiences we have been examining found their first inspiration there.

Let us close, then, by thinking of some of the things which emerge from His Life and teaching. Prayer, said Jesus, must be "in faith". It must be real, and based in a sense of reality. It must be "in secret" that is, coming from the deeper, inner part of our nature—the shut door and the inner chamber are, above all else, pictures of a state of mind: the clamour, preoccupations, motives and cares of the world are shut out for the time being. It must be "in my name". This is the kind of prayer of which we have just been thinking: prayer made in accordance with His Spirit, His purpose, His outlook: made, indeed, on the ground of His Redemption. It is not prayer uttered "with the requisite formula attached", but prayer rising right out of our discipleship, uttered because we are His and out of concern for Him and His Kingdom, inspired by His Spirit.

He Himself affords the greatest examples of a man praying. Though He was God come amongst us, He lived a fully human life, dependent all the time upon His heavenly Father. He addressed the Father "in heaven", and knew the heavenly realm as the sphere of power and full knowledge. One notices about His praying a deep element of thanksgiving. One notices His prayers for His men, and His looking to God when about to perform an act of healing. We find Him praying at times of crisis. There are indications scattered throughout the records which enable us to understand how He depended upon this living contact with God.

Especially impressive are the model prayer which He gave to His disciples, and the prayer which He prayed in the Upper Room. That prayer in John 17 is full of petition, emphasising that it is uttered in the spirit of dependence from the realm of earth to the Father in heaven. In it, indeed, we find Jesus asking for things which we might have thought—He being who He is—that there was no need to ask for ("Glorify thou me", He prays in verse 5, "with the glory I had with thee before the world was"—there is nothing purely automatic about this!). In verse 24 we find Him definitely expressing His will: "I will that they also, whom thou hast given me, be with me where I am." Prayer is the expression of a human will, lit by the knowledge of God's will, abiding in the Father and initiating things uttered in faith. Above everything else, this prayer from the Upper Room shines as an example of communion with the Father. Full of urgent and compelling petition, its nature is yet that of communion: a dialogue of which we only have the words said from this side of reality by the human Jesus. In God's presence, the Son is thinking, and planning, and expressing His Will.

There is a "school of Prayer" into which all may enter.

Ever since the first disciples uttered the cry, "Lord, teach us to pray," it has been the appropriate word for the Christians of each succeeding generation.

All those at whom we have been looking learned their lessons first of all from Him. None of them, in any of these matters, have gone beyond Him. All they have discovered is a little more light on His own experience, and on the things He had to say. What has happened is that these things have come alive for them. They have entered—as we are invited to enter— a little further into our possibilities in Christ.

ACKNOWLEDGMENTS and BIBLIOGRAPHY

Grateful thanks are accorded to these authors and publishers for the necessary permission to quote from their works, and also to Miss Helen Macnicol for permission to quote her father's translation of N. V. Tilak's hymn on pp.118–19. Special thanks are also accorded to Miss Muriel Lester, Dr. A. Skevington Wood, and the Rev. and Mrs. Tom Dring.

HUGH REDWOOD:

Residue of Days
                Hodder & Stoughton   1958
Practical Prayer
                Hodder & Stoughton   1937
Bristol Fashion
                Marshall, Morgan & Scott   1948

EDWIN ORR:

Can God—? (15th Edition revised).
                Marshall, Morgan & Scott   1951
The Second Evangelical Awakening in Britain
                Marshall, Morgan & Scott   —

STANLEY JONES:

Abundant Living
        Abingdon Press, New York & Hodder & Stoughton 1946
Mastery
        Abingdon Press, New York & Hodder & Stoughton 1956
The Christ of Every Road
        Abingdon Press, New York & Hodder & Stoughton 1930
The Way
        Abingdon Press, New York & Hodder & Stoughton 1947

GLENN CLARK:

On Wings of Prayer
                Arthur James (Evesham)   1956

ACKNOWLEDGMENTS AND BIBLIOGRAPHY

I Will Lift Up Mine Eyes
> Arthur James (Evesham) 1953

The Lord's Prayer
> Macalester Park Publishing Co., St. Paul,
> Minn. 1932

How to find Health through Prayer
> Harper & Bros., New York 1940
> Arthur James (Evesham) 1955

MURIEL LESTER:

It occurred to me
> (Printed privately) 1936

Ways of Praying
> Independent Press 1931

Praying: How, When, Where and Why
> Independent Press 1956

FLORENCE ALLSHORN:

Florence Allshorn, by J. H. Oldham   S.C.M. 1951
The Notebooks of Florence Allshorn, selected and arranged by
a member of St. Julian's Community, S.C.M. 1957

AMY CARMICHAEL:

Gold Cord
> The Dohnavur Fellowship (Agents: S.P.C.K.) 1932

Windows
> The Dohnavur Fellowship (Agents: S.P.C.K.) 1937

Amy Carmichael, by Frank Houghton
> The Dohnavur Fellowship (Agents: S.P.C.K.) 1951

MALCOLM SPENCER:

God's Back-room Boy, by McEwan Lawson
> Lutterworth Press 1952
Thanksgiving—The Key to Prayer S.C.M. 1927
Vitality S.C.M. 1931

STUDDERT KENNEDY:

When we Pray, by Ronald Sinclair
> Hodder & Stoughton 1932

REBECCA BEARD:

Everyman's Search
> Arthur James (Evesham) 1951

Everyman's Adventure
>> Arthur James (Evesham)   1956

PAUL CLAUDEL:

Lord Teach us to Pray, tr. Ruth Bethell.
>> Dennis Dobson   1947
The Correspondence 1899–1926 *between Paul Claudel and André Gide*, tr. John Russell
>> Secker & Warburg   1952

LILIAN BAYLIS:

Lilian Baylis, by Sybil and Russell Thorndike
>> Chapman & Hall   1938

FRANK LAUBACH:

Prayer—the Mightiest Force in the World
>> Fleming H. Revell, New York and Lutterworth Press   1946
Letters of a Modern Mystic
>> Lutterworth Press   1937
Channels of Spiritual Power
>> Lutterworth Press   1955
The Master Speaks
>> Arthur James (Evesham)   1956

JACK WINSLOW:

Eyelids of the Dawn
>> Hodder & Stoughton   1954
When I Awake
>> Hodder & Stoughton   —

C. F. ANDREWS:

What I Owe to Christ
>> Hodder & Stoughton   1932
The Inner Life
>> Hodder & Stoughton   1939

FORBES ROBINSON:

Letters to His Friends (Printed privately)
General Gordon, by Lord Elton
>> Collins   1954

ACKNOWLEDGMENTS AND BIBLIOGRAPHY

BILLY GRAHAM:

The Billy Graham Story, by C. T. Cook
Marshall, Morgan & Scott   1954

ALEXIS CARREL:

Prayer, tr. C. J. Wright
Hodder & Stoughton   1947
Man the Unknown
Hamish Hamilton   1935

LESLIE WEATHERHEAD:

Psychology, Religion and Healing
Hodder & Stoughton   1951

OSWALD CHAMBERS:

The Discipline of Prayer
Oswald Chambers Publications (Agents:
Marshall, Morgan & Scott)   1936
My Utmost for His Highest
Oswald Chambers Publications (Agents:
Marshall, Morgan & Scott)   1927
"If ye shall ask . . ."
Oswald Chambers Publications (Agents:
Marshall, Morgan & Scott)   1937
Oswald Chambers: His Life and Work
Oswald Chambers Publications (Agents:
Marshall, Morgan & Scott)   1933

THOMAS H. KELLY:

A Testament of Devotion
Hodder & Stoughton   1943